Gaps of Brightness

By the same author

All Cultivated People: A History of the United Arts Club

Contents

1 In the family fold

I TOOK IT PERFECTLY SERIOUSLY when some joker called Coalisland the Venice of the North. It is the town where I was born, in 1913, the tenth of twelve children— Martin, Molly, Daniel, Phauds, Jack, Nina, Basil, James, Mena, me, Joe and Kevin. I was so young when I left Coalisland that it stays in my mind only as a dream place. It glimmers in the waters of the canal which opened out into the Basin in the middle of the town.

The Basin. A flat factual name for the only baptism of grace given to an otherwise mean straggle of street and houses. Yet it

A St Patrick's Day parade in 'the Venice of the North'

[3]

was the heart and soul of the town. It gave height and depth and wavering life to the few buildings reflected in it. It was mitred by heavy chains, ready-made swings for children.

Stewart's Mill, a grey mass of solid stone, dominated the Basin. A wide jetty projected from it. Black barges from Belfast, laden with golden cargo, millions of nuggets of yellow maize, nudged black walls and discharged their showers of sun-shot hail into bags for grinding in the mill. It was a forbidden delight for us youngsters to sit on the edge of the hold when the hatch was opened and with bare feet to kick up a spray of glittering grain until the men from the mill lowered the level of the water in the lock, moving the barge below our reach. 'The line', as the tow-path was called, bordered the canal leading out of the Basin. Big, strong horses heaved and strained towing the barges to the lock which released them on to the canal on their journey towards Lough Neagh.

In the spring the water-bailiff's garden was lit by laburnum which trailed branches in the water, and heavily tasselled lilac glowed gently in a fragrant torpor. All summer long the water at the lock churned with brave high divers and thrashing swimmers. A Regatta was the highlight of summer when people came from near and far to compete in swimming and diving contests, punting races, to be first to cross the greasy pole or just to jeer and cheer in equal measure at the efforts of the hapless competitors. Sadism was out for the day and got its tuppence worth from the unseemly gyrations of young fellows hiding their shame as they dressed or undressed under slipping towels. Some spread-eagled flatly into the water in a dive meant to display the flight of a bird. Shouts of encouragement for frantic efforts to keep a hold on the greasy pole kept a winner going until his hands and arms gave way to legs and crossed ankles till he fell to the bank and the crowd cheered his due.

The punting competition was the comedy act. Laughter as much as want of skill drove the 'punts', a home-made collection of unbiddable craft, into collisions and crazy zigzag passage from bank to bank. Broom handles interlocked and rafts turned over, canting their crews. It seems that only men and boys took part. It was a show for the girls, dressed in summery best who fell on each other in helpless mirth as they watched.

In autumn secret romances ripened and couples were spied walking the tow-path, 'doing a line'. In winter, when the frost was hard and lasted long enough, skating on the Basin gave a startling airiness and gaiety to 'holy Jaysus' who owned the brick-yard and to wee 'Baby Quinn' who could dig a body's garden as well as any man, as they curled over the frozen water. All this carry-on passed our grandmother, our father's mother, by. She lived up the town, near the chapel and was 'doting'.

I remember her only from the fact that my sister Mena and I, the youngest of the four girls in our family of twelve, were given the duty to call on her on Sundays after Mass. She would have attended, dressed in a black cape with jet beads sewed in a pattern over the shoulders, with a jet-trimmed bonnet to match. She maintained that the grandfather clock in the hall tick-tocked the name of the curate: 'Father Cush, Father Cush. Father Cush, Father Cush . . . ' She insisted on giving us our breakfast of bacon and egg and potato cake and insulted us by serving it on one plate between the two of us. It was not made more palatable by Mena's pushing raw yolk to my side, or, for her, by my trying to rid my side of transparent white to her side. We did our best to eat what bacon and potato cake was not contaminated by the raw egg and to drink the strong sweet tea she gave us. Father Cush was good to her and Mother hinted that Father and he had an 'arrange-ment'. He saw to it that she had a good front seat at any concert, or play, or laughable farce that travelling players brought to the town. The first moving film shown in St Patrick's Hall was a sen-sation not least because Grandmother became hysterical when one of the characters was shot.

Basil, Nina, Mena and James

'Get the doctor! Get the doctor!' she screamed, violently pushing her neighbour.

I don't remember when she died but she lives on in a picture in my head of a little black figure with a halo of glitter, arms flailing in rings round her.

Initiation

A long bed of nettles grew at the bottom of a grassy hill behind our house. A sort of ceremony of initiation that younger brothers and sisters and cousins had to undergo to admit them to group enterprises such as tree climbing, or bird nesting, was, I suppose, a painful introduction to elders' duplicity. The victim was taken to the top of the hill, wrapped tightly in a rug, swung to and fro to a gentle rhythm, then suddenly tipped out to roll down the hill into the nettles. The crushed weeds were harmless but the flattened path out of the bed had to be negotiated with a care for the rogues which sprang to life and viciously stung bare legs and ankles as if in revenge for the assault on them.

Only the most penetrating wails induced one or other of the sadists to come to the rescue and lift the novice to safety. The agony, of course, was just beginning as the stings burned like red-

Mother posing in her wedding dress,
holding her ivory and ostrich feather fan

hot needles. Guilt and fear of discovery with a touch of sympathy set the culprits to work with dock leaves to cool the skin and ease the pain. The cure was more psychological than scientific partly due to unwonted attention and partly to the determination of the patient to share mysterious dangers plotted in secret. Such a one was a quiet lure of Mrs Beatty's black ass from its open stable to give bare-back rides, in turn, 'down the road'. Getting the animal to trot, never mind gallop, won respect and deference for the rider.

Market day in Dungannon

In cold weather the kitchen was the warmest place in the house. It was there that the youngest of us were made presentable for special occasions so it must have been in late autumn or early winter that we moved to Dungannon. My Sunday petticoats were hung to air on the back of a chair near the range. First to go on was one of crocheted wool, tied at the waist by a lace of the same wool, slotted through the tatted edge. Next was one of calico, a proper one with a bodice edged with narrow lace and over that went a white cambric underskirt sporting a flounce of broderie anglaise.

Try as I might I cannot remember what else I wore that day, but I do remember being wrapped in a rug and handed up to someone sitting high on a sidecar with nothing that I could see to prevent my falling except the arm of a big brother. I must have gone fast asleep because I woke in a bed in a strange room with Mena asleep beside me. Our new house on the market square was strategically sited to command a view of the activities of the town and its inhabitants.

To go to Dungannon for a day was a treat. To go there to live was almost too good to be true. We soon learned that the nuns in the convent school were just as demanding as Master Kelly had been in the National School in Coalisland. The blissful difference was that the route through the square, especially on market day, was a school in itself but with a world of difference. Thursday was market day in Dungannon as it had been for four hundred years and more. Queen Elizabeth the First, herself, raised Hugh O'Neill to the Earldom of Tyrone and granted him a charter to hold a weekly market on Thursdays and it became 'the market day', when people gathered from all over the county.

Early in the morning the stalls were set out in spacious rows. They were strongly made, their counters enclosed on two sides by wooden walls which supported pitched roofs of corrugated iron. They had sedan handles for easy transport. All bare and clean they looked like little houses in a new estate and then, in jig time, they were possessed by their laughing, eager tenants.

The old clothes woman quickly secured her lines high round her stall. In minutes it was a pirate ship in miniature, its sails of myriad colours bellying in the wind and bearing the plunder of as many fashion forecasts. A hedge of old suits was hardly sufficient insulation against the passionate entreaties of the pot and pan man to buy 'while they lasted,' his bargain lots. Strings of sparkling tins in jangling dangles played accompaniment to the dull cacophony of enamel ware, the short sharp explosion of broken glass and the reverberations of an upset pile of buckets. A stack of plates, 'hardly a chip out of one o' them' would go for 'nothin' or next it,' with a nice wee blue-band bowl thrown in for luck. But he'd take 'Nothin' less than the marked price, m'am', for the china hen sitting on her barren nest.

Mounds of oranges blazed for the morning and sank with the setting sun. Java, tangerine, Seville and speckled blood oranges sold singly, by the dozen, by the penn'orth for the slightly damaged and, later in the day, for nothing at all to the bare-footed boys who'd scramble for them. The sweet stall's honey-combed mounds of 'yalla man', its black knots of glossy liquorice laces, the glass jars of bulls' eyes and dolly mixture and jelly babies were so many magnets to us. Somehow the same confections were not so desperately desirable behind a plate glass window as now when a stranger woman doled them out in penny lumps or counted them into hot grubby hands.

The Spanish Onion

All the sights and sounds of the market coloured the eye and tuned the ear but what tickled my fancy always was the Spanish Onion. He was a small man, as lithe and as sharp as a whip. His face was yellow and his hair was red and, although he was no young fellow, his teeth were white as the inside of an onion. He set his stage by laying out his big Spanish onions in a ring around him on the ground. Then, commanding attention, he would call out in a sing-song, 'Ate an onion an' earn a bob, a rale bob. On'y the best Spanish onions aten in this contest. On'y boys can compate, a bob t'winner, the first t' finish his onion.'

He would barely have time to draw breath before a rush of

boys had taken possession, each of his onion, sitting cross-legged like tailors in a circle on the cobbles. With great deliberation the master of ceremonies did the round with a jack-knife, topping and tailing. The boys turned their noses this way and that to escape the smarting fumes as they tore at the papery jackets. The Spanish Onion danced, demented. He prodded them between shoulder blades. He signalled like a tic-tac man at the races and called on the growing audience to lay a bet on a winner. 'Bite an'swally! Bite an' swally!' he'd urge the competitors, beating the air in encouragement.

By this time they were in no condition to heed him. Water gushed from their eyes and juice dripped from their mouths. They took big tearing bites and chewed hard with teeth bared and eyes screwed tight. After each struggling gulp of a swallow they'd groan or cry out or sigh or sob out a froth of little bubbles while foamy dribbles of chewed pulp speckled their jerseys. The tinsmith's son from Shamble Lane was a champion 'swallier'. He earned the money hard but he wanted it badly and generally he got it. Away he'd run in the direction of home, spitting as he ran, clutching his shilling and sped by the laughter and applause of the satisfied punters at the ringside.

The Spanish Onion, without ever a word to the prostrated defeated, then dodged nimbly through the crowd, holding open his green baize bag and touting for new victims.

'Ah paid the bob, sir. The wee fella wi' the grey shirt (or the brown coat or the red jersey) got the bob, sir. Help wi' the prize-money sir. Another onion atin' contest in fifteen minutes. On'y the best Spanish onions used in this consarn. Good for the health, the teeth, the hair an' t'eyes. Ate an onion an'earn a bob, a silver bob wi' the king's head on it. Help t'make up the prize money, sir,' and he'd waltz away to a group of townsmen haggling with a farmer over the price of a cart-load of turnips.

On a very few days during the year differences of politics and religions cast a shadow of blight over the town but never on market days. No one was concerned with what colour they were, orange or green, or what foot they dug with, left or right. Politics and religion hung fire for one day in the week and all passed the time of day as if they were the best of friends and never a difference between them. Watching for who came into town was a regular pastime for some that had nothing better to do. The triplets Sarah, Maisie and Nora Horan gave them more satisfaction than most. You couldn't miss them. People made way as the three of them cut through the crowds. I watched the idlers watching them and long afterwards I took them out of the corner they occupied of my memory of Market Day and turned them into a short story.

The triplets

It was understood that the triplets, Sarah, Maisie, and Nora Horan were a little bit simple-minded. Maybe they were and maybe they weren't but it was true that they were innocent for their age. Their mother died while they were still young girls and they led a lonely life with their father, Willie John. He was the Canon's gardener, so anyone who stepped out of line with them knew that the Canon would have it in for him. He kept an eye on them and gave them odd jobs around the presbytery and church to keep them occupied but, even so, without regular work they had time on their hands.

It upset them to be separated. One wouldn't work without the others, wouldn't even try, so with the best will in the world, and with all his influence, even the Canon found it hard to make work for three where one would do. Willie John must have been partly responsible for their oddities for he treated them as if they were the age they had been when his wife died, and never seemed to realise that they were women now, tall and strong and forty if they were a day.

They lived in a funny wee house in the demesne. It was turreted like a toy castle and had narrow arched windows filled with thick lumpy panes of green glass. Black barbered yew trees stood guard all round it. The girls all dressed the same in jumpers they knitted them-

selves, trimmed with lace bertha collars, white cotton gloves, and buttoned boots. Their pepper-and-salt tweed skirts were their only concession to fashion. They took them up or let them down according to the dictates of the day. In winter or bad weather they wore men's tweed caps, and raincoats their father got for them from surplus British army uniforms.

No one admired their hair more than they did themselves. It was thick and long and a lovely brown colour with golden lights, got, they would tell if asked, from never washing in anything but rainwater. They wore it in plaits with big black velvet bows tying it back on the crown of their heads and small bows at the ends to secure them. The plaits were long enough to sit on and they bobbed about as the girls twisted this way and that to see all they could on the stalls or leaned into the backs of carts to see where a couple of bonhams were squealing after being sold away from their sow.

They loved to be noticed and never minded if some smart alec passed a remark such as 'God-a-God but yer lukin' rightly the day,' or winked at them. They nudged each other and giggled and looked away and carried on wending their way round the Square. They usually ended their tour at Reynold's grocery shop and McGinty's Emporium when one or other of them went into Reynold's to buy sixpence worth of broken biscuits and a large bottle of lemonade. The three would stand in a huddle outside the shop poking through the bag to see if they were in luck with plenty of pieces of chocolate covered shortcake, wafers and coconut creams before setting off with them for home.

One market day they went as usual to visit McGinty's Emporium. It had separate departments for the different kinds of goods but the triplets always made for fabrics. They came every week for 'pattrins'. One particular day they were taken aback to see a new apprentice behind the counter. They knew Doney Harper. Doney was part of their lives, important in the rituals of their day in the town. They called him Mr Harper and when they asked him for 'pattrins' of a material he would snip tiny bits off the chosen bolts and hand them over. The girls passed them to each other, held them up to catch the light from the window and made great show of comparing colours.

'Take your time now. Sure there's no hurry,' Doney always told them.

After a whispered conversation they would ask Mr Harper to hold the chosen bolt over till the next market day when 'Dada' would have seen the 'pattrins'. It was, of course, the same story over and over again but Doney never let on that he had heard it before. The sisters were wary of McCutcheon, the new apprentice. They tried not to notice that he wasn't Doney Harper and carried on as usual inspecting bolts of cloth and asking for patterns of the ones they liked. He decided that he wasn't going to waste time on this lot who, by the look of them, had neither the intention nor the means to buy anything; but there was nothing to stop him from getting a bit of fun out of them.

It was his misfortune that they were in a bad humour for, in addition to the shock of the disappearance of Mr Harper, they were disappointed. All they had got for their sixpence in Reynold's was a bag of pieces of cream crackers, bits of plain tea biscuits and a few cracked ginger snaps; nothing covered with chocolate, or with a cream filling, and no pink wafers.

'Give us a lock o'yer hair an' ah'll give ye all the pattrins ye want,' McCutcheon smirked in response to Maisie's request.

He leaned across the counter and tugged her plait. The big scissors for cutting cloth were lying on the counter. Maisie eyed them. Picked them up. She pulled her plait over her shoulder, cut it off and threw it at him. Nora took the scissors from Maisie and copied her exactly. Sarah looked at her sisters, frightened and delighted. She held out her plait to Nora who obligingly cut it off. They looked at each other, clapped their hands to their faces, aghast, with a dawning realisation of what they had done.

They shook their heads like dervishes. They shrieked, grabbed their plaits, threw them at McCutcheon. The little bows fell off. The lovely shining hair loosened and fell all over him. It stuck to his hands and got into his mouth as he tried to beat it off but he was half blinded and the triplets' blood was up. Maisie swivelled herself over the counter and held him. Nora followed to help her while Sarah possessed the scissors and lay on her stomach on the counter to reach the half fainting McCutcheon held by her sisters.

She lifted his hair in tufts and cut to the scalp with quiet grunts of satisfaction as Maisie and Nora guided her to any stray wisps she missed. The three worked with intense concentration as if trained as a team for the job.

McGinty, on patrol around his shop, heard McCutcheon's yelps as Maisie nicked the skin of his scalp when she cut too close. He came running. He could never explain how he did it, for he was no athlete, but he vaulted the counter and violently shoved his apprentice out of the girls' grasp and herded them, mewing like cats awanting, into his office. He shouted to Miss Toner in Haberdashery to go at once for Willie John and the Canon. It seemed an age till they came. McGinty was beside himself, near hysterics. He dunted Willie John in the back.

'Look at them! Look at them! They're docile now but, my God, they were savage. Would ye look at the cut of them? Wouldn't ye be heart sore at the sight o' them?'

Willie John stretched his arms around them.

'Shoosh. Shoosh now. Dada's here. Ssh. There's the good girls,' and he stroked the heads nuzzling into his chest.

The Canon flapped his hands.

'Stop it,' he commanded. 'That's enough. Stop the girnin', ye'll upset your poor father. Away home with ye and say your prayers. The morra's another day and we'll all be the better for it.'

'They haven't a tither o' wit between the lot o' them,' he addressed Willie John. 'Take the trap and get them home out of this before the whole town's in on us. Give them their supper and get them to bed and I'll have a word with ye later. Ye won't be hard on them but ye know well yourself, Willie John, it's time they were settled.'

He got the nuns to take them into the convent as lay sisters to *mind the poultry and help in the garden. They didn't mind a bit having the rest of their hair cut off to accommodate their veils which hung down their backs just as their plaits used to do. Reverend Mother reported that they were perfectly happy and surprisingly good at gardening so long as they were left alone and kept hard at it.*

McCutcheon went up to Belfast to stay with an aunt for a while and then he went to Canada. He was quiet in himself when he came home for a holiday a year or so later. His hair had grown piebald. He didn't stay long. Maybe he got tired of being asked for 'pattrins'.

I never forgot the Indian and his queer headgear. In time he, too, became a short story.

The Indian

The Indian always came to the town on the market day before Christmas. He was a scourge to Matt Killen who suspected the man's motives for straying so far from his own place. Matt wanted no truck with foreigners. His wife, Jinny, had a different view. She chipped away at Matt's prejudice until, after years of effort, he capitulated under the delusion that taking on the Indian was solely his idea.

The rich brown hams hanging on a wall in Matt's shop at Christmas time harmonised well with the ivory skins and yellow legs of turkeys hung from hooks under a shelf near the door where a strong draught kept them cool. The purply red wattles made lively daubs of colour so that the turkeys didn't look quite so dead. Long candles for lighting in windows on Christmas Eve to assure the Holy Family of a welcome, should they come looking for shelter, were stowed into bags and boxes and baskets as Mrs Killen took orders.

A wheel of yellow cheese bolstered sides and rolls of bacon beside the slicing machine that only she could manage. Boxes of dried and candied fruit from exotic places like Greece and Italy and Morocco, displayed on ledges on a raked board, reminded everyone that it was cake and pudding time again. Customers crowding in brought trails of frosty air, making a mist in the heat given out by the big-bellied stove at the back of the shop.

The heat, the haze, and the smells excited the women and loosened their purses as well as their tongues. They abandoned their lists and if one bought two pounds of fancy biscuits, mixed, another would best her and buy a whole tin. Mrs Killen envied them their freedom to buy what they liked and often wished she had money of her own such as the egg money the farmers' wives saved for themselves to spend on market days and holidays. It never occurred to Matt that she might want for anything with everything under her hand. She stifled vague longings for some change that would, maybe, sometimes give her a laugh. All the same, she thanked God while she weighed and wrapped and sliced, that Matt was steady and sober at the end of the day and, if she played her cards right, he would agree to the Christmas decorations.

'Leave that fancy business t' the twins,' he said crossly to her when she asked for money to buy two paper streamers, two lanterns and a package of doilys from the Indian. Twin sisters ran a cake shop two doors up from Matt's. They were a thorn in his side with their prissy ways and high-falutin' notions and it was no recommendation that they were the Indian's best customers. They loved his highly coloured sparkly boxes and his little brass bowls and vases and they always bought a supply of paper doilys from him to set off their cakes and pastries.

Matt gave in to Mrs Killen on the streamers and the lanterns but doilys he would not tolerate. He hung the streamers from the four corners of the ceiling, crossing them in the middle, and who knows what secret joy he got from the hanging of them for he always insisted on doing the job himself. Mrs Killen hung one lantern in the middle of the window and it wasn't once, but several times, that she nipped across the road to the chemist's for the pleasure of looking at it on the way back. The other was to give to Father Malachy to hang over the crib in the chapel on the understanding that he prayed for her special intention. She leaned half-a-dozen packets of doilys against the slab-

cake at the sweetie end of the counter in the hope that Matt wouldn't notice them. She reasoned that if they went well and made money she might be let keep a packet for herself. She had asked the twins to get them for her, along with the streamers and lanterns, from the Indian, for Matt wouldn't have him in the shop and he wouldn't have the doilies either.

'Doilys, for God's sake,' he shouted when he saw them. 'Doilys how are ye! Airs an' graces!'

He swept the packet into the zinc bath under the counter holding bad oranges, cabbage leaves and broken eggs. He had rough ways and a rough tongue, but people knew that there was no real harm in him. Anyway, his eggs were always fresh, his vegetables clean and his potatoes well sorted. His bacon was the best in the town for it was properly cured and only oak shavings, got from the coffin maker, were used for the smoking of it. He was in his element in his shop keeping up a commentary of greeting and gossip.

'Hell t'yer sowl m'am an' is it yerself? Ah heard tell himself got a great price for the piebald he sold t' the Brothers. More power t'im. Move over there m'am till ah lower a ham for Mrs. Nulty. That ham came from Birney an' no man ever kept better animals than the same Birney. It's been three months in the curin'—twelve pounds weight. Ye'll tik it? God knows ye'll need it with that crowd ye have t'feed.'

He touched Mrs Killen's ankle with the toe of his boot, his cue to her to put an extra pound of tea with Mrs Nulty's order as a mark of respect for the size of her family and for being a loyal customer through the year. He knew every farmer in the county but had never been farther than Coagh in his life which may have been the reason for his jealousy of the Indian. What would bring a body from the other side of the world if he wasn't up to something? The man's headgear and his sing-songy accent irritated him. And why should he bow and scrape the way he did if there wasn't some ploy at the back of it? He must be up to some divilment to come all the way from the back of beyond to this place. Whatever it was it wasn't going to catch on in Dungannon if Matt could help it. The town was all right the way it was. It needed no foreigners putting notions into people's heads.

'Doilys,' he muttered. 'Oney the beginnin'.'

The Indian was a small smiling man. His teeth shone whitely in his dark face. There was no knowing how old he was but he was certainly over fifty from the grey wisps of hair that escaped his saffron coloured turban. There was a soft light in his chocolate eyes and he spoke to the twins with an insistent anxious rhythm.

'These new stock. I sell only you. Put in window. Now is time. Presents for mammies, for aunties, for little children. My vases for flowers very nice. One on table food taste better. You like my bowls? Solid brass, madam. These boxes. Are they not beautiful? See the shine. To keep things safe. Not lose them. Rings. Cuff-links. You like? You buy? I not come again long time. Maybe never.'

He laid out his wares on the lid of the wooden box he carried them in, secured by broad leather straps across his shoulders and clasped in front to a belt round his waist. The twins fingered them, turned them upside down, looked inside, tried lids for fit, held them up to eye-level, put a few of them aside and made an all-in offer. The Indian knew the drill and to save face, he made his usual useless protest.

'Is not good price. What can I do? My wife, my children, they must eat. I too must live . . .' and, sadly, with downcast eyes, he agreed a price a little above the twins' offer.

He took doilys from a canvas bag hooked to the back of his belt. They were lovely white lacy things in three sizes. The twins chose a number of packages and took it for granted that the price was as it had always been although it had gone up little by little to the Indian over the years; but, still, he made a small profit and he had not the energy to argue with these good businesswomen whom he admired.

'See you next time round,' they called as he left the shop. They wouldn't have dreamed of shaking hands with him. He was 'the Indian'. They never asked him his name. No one in the town did. There were millions like him in India. A huge country. Very poor. He was lucky to be out of it. Even if his suit and shoes were on the *shabby side. long past their best, wouldn't he be in his bare feet, probably, if he had stayed where he belonged?*

He steadied himself on his bicycle at the kerb, wobbled as he balanced the box on his back and pedalled off to Pomeroy to cajole a customer he had there:

'I sell only you. Presents for mammies . . . You like? You buy? My wife . . . My children . . . '

Matt Killen glimpsed him as he spun past the shop. An idea came into his head. There must be money in the knick-knacks the Indian sold in the town. For one thing, the women were mad about them. What else would keep him cycling all over the county in all weathers? He'd been at it a long time now and wouldn't it be only natural if he stopped and stayed in the one place if he got the chance and could make a living in it? That wooden box with the inlaid brass Jinny had bought from him was a well-made piece worth ten times the price if only he had a bit of wit. He had told the twins that it had come from his place in India where the whole population worked at making such things and that was why it had come so cheap. The important thing in business, Matt reminded himself, was to be sure of a ready supply of stock of consistent quality and that, by all accounts, the Indian had.

Mrs Curley, a widow, lived next door to the Killens. They were very good to her since the last of her three sons had taken off to join the two others in America and left her with only the cat for company. She was well over eighty. Lately, her health had begun to fail since she got dizzy one day and fell and broke her hip. She was being kept in the infirmary until the weather improved and she could be out and about again. When Mrs Killen went to see her and brought her her clean night-dresses and calves' foot jelly with port, she doubted, by the look of her, that the poor woman would leave the infirmary alive nor did the Matron encourage her to think that she might.

Matt was sorry to hear it. He liked Mrs Curley. He hoped she had her affairs in order and smiled to himself for he knew them well. She paid him half-a-crown a month against the cost of the new roof he'd put on her house for her a year ago. He took the money, more to save her feelings than from any hope that the bill would ever be paid off. If and when she died he would be out of pocket a fair bit. He saw no harm, so, in putting a wee plan he had into action.

He would get Gault, the solicitor, to write to the three sons, if he could find them, to tell them about their mother's condition. He would make a fair offer for the mother's house to whichever of them turned up. In the meantime he'd ask the matron to encourage Mrs Curley to make her will. She was sensible enough and would enjoy the importance of settling her estate. She need never know that everything she possessed would barely cover her funeral expenses, never mind what she owed him. He was satisfied that, one way or another, the house was his, or would be in due course.

He looked up admiringly at the paper streamers and across at the Chinese lantern in the window softly glowing from the candle so carefully placed in the wire holder inside and, with growing regret, at the doilys in the zinc bath, destroyed by a broken egg. The shop was doing well. He was making good money. There was nothing to stop him from expanding the way McGinty had when he bought the old flax mill and joined it to what he liked to call his establishment.

Mrs Curley's house would make a lovely wee shop. McGinty called his enlarged premises an EMPORIUM. He would have a bazaar. His mind raced. KILLEN'S INDIAN BAZAAR! He would keep it apart from the main shop and he would fill it with the stuff people had to go to Belfast for as well as the kind of goods the Indian sold. He would put the Indian in charge. He was a hard worker. The turban thing he wore on his head was just the ticket to attract custom. He'd get the town handyman, McCabe, to convert the three upstairs rooms in Mrs Curley's house into living quarters for him. The man would be better off than he ever was in his life before; and if he told the truth and had a wife and children didn't they live on top of each other, anyway, where he came from?

Mrs Curley died in the middle of January. None of the sons turned up for the funeral. The two that Gault had been able to contact sent money for wreaths and masses and their letters explained good reasons why they couldn't come. They were glad to accept Matt's offer of a couple of hundred pounds made, for decency's sake, through Gault, for their mother's place.

Gault found the Indian in Enniskillen and drove him back to Dungannon to discuss Matt's plans for the bazaar. He turned out to be a far better businessman than they took him for. He produced a solicitor of his own, Asdir Amin, to examine the partnership contract and to add a few addenda on behalf of Rajput Alashi, a different man altogether from the one they had known as 'the Indian'. His wife turned out to be a small plump woman from Galway. When Rajput paid her the most extravagant compliments she shook like a jelly with silent laughter and her two young daughters laughed too even though they didn't know what they were laughing at, no more than did Mrs Killen when she joined in.

The two families became good friends. Rajput told them so many stories about the splendours and wonders of India that Matt began to have notions of seeing them for himself; but, Jinny, his wife, soon put a stop to them.

'If you go, I go, and who'll mind the shop?' There was no answer to that so Matt contented himself with planning a grand opening of KILLEN'S INDIAN BAZAAR on the Market Day before Christmas to catch the crowds. Canon Quinn was the first customer. He bought an inlaid copper tray as a hansel, he said, instead of a blessing so as not to offend Rajput's religious convictions, whatever they were. He welcomed the family to the town and remarked that Dungannon was becoming quite cosmopolitan.

The Corrs

Our cousins, the Corrs, lived in a large house among trees called The Retreat. On summer evenings our Aunt Annie, my father's sister, sat under a tree and called her five daughters, one by one, to have their hair brushed the regulation hundred strokes. She was ten years older than her husband, John Corr, and when she died he described her as his 'adored wife' in the newspaper death notice. The crows called 'Corr, Corr. Corr, Corr' as they settled into the trees during those long balmy evenings.

Our Uncle Johnny was a solicitor who became the county registrar. He dressed formally in black jacket, striped trousers, white shirt, high starched collar with turned down corners and widely knotted black tie. He was a tall, quiet, gentle man, and his habitual benign expression inspired affection and trust while his status ensured respect. And he was a fair man for much as he loved his family and adored Aunt Annie he comforted me once when my cousins sent me to Coventry. I forgot their instructions to me, by then a young teenager, to dance only with Pat McGrory at one of their parties. They reserved the two tall sons of the chemist in Maghera for themselves; but when one and then the other invited me to dance I was only too delighted to comply and never noticed the baleful looks the cousins directed at me. By this time we lived four miles away in Dungannon and so, on this occasion, my sisters and I stayed the night at The Retreat. At breakfast I was at first puzzled and then hurt when the cousins refused to speak to me and pointedly moved milk and sugar, bread and butter, and a dish of boiled eggs out of my reach. I met Uncle Johnny on the stairs as I went up, crying, to my room.

'What? What?' he exclaimed. 'Crying! We can't have this. Tell me now. What's the matter?' and he put his arm around my shoulder.

'They won't talk to me,' I blurted. 'I should've danced with Pat McGroary and I didn't.'

'Now who'd want to dance with wee Pat McGrory? Don't mind

them. They're jealous but they'll get over it,' he said kindly and patted my cheek.

The thought of my cousins being jealous of me cheered me up no end and as they had had the satisfaction of making me cry grievances were soon forgotten. Anyhow, the main attraction of the parties was the food. It was plentiful and it looked scrump-

Martin, the first of the family, aged about eighteen months

tious. There were rabbit and fish-shaped terrines; colourful cooked vegetables layered and patterned in aspic; potato and rice salads dappled with herbs; tomato salad; lettuce salad with scallions, hard-boiled egg and radish; blancmanges and jellies turreted or patterned according to the moulds they had set in.

There were platters of chicken, ham, and tongue, but what I waited and longed for was a slice of any one of the three large plum cakes, placed in a row at equal distance from each other down the middle of the long table. They were topped with inch-high almond icing and decorated with clusters of life-like marzipan fruits. When I politely said No to a helping of something or other, I would prefer a piece of plum cake, Mena muttered crossly, 'It wouldn't be you if you didn't put your foot in it.' Those cakes never were cut so far as I could see. I believe they weren't real at all, but artificial, put on show party after party.

Food for twelve

Daily diet at home had three certainties: it was different from one day to the next; whatever it was it looked lovely and it tasted good; my problem was to get my share of the goodies. I was the tenth in line, and as the two below me were boys, Joe and Kevin, and usually in a desperate hurry, I was often the last to be served and left to wonder if there would be anything at all for me. There always was, of course, and I had the advantage of getting to scrape the dishes of delicious crisp or toffyish leavings.

Feeding twelve was no joke. There had to be quantity and quality and the cost had to be reasonable. There was no end to our mother's ingenuity. It was one thing she had plenty of and, looking back, she must have enjoyed being the mother of necessity. She had great respect for food and could get better value from potatoes, say, or from a cabbage than any professional cook. With Bridget—'the girl'—to help her she'd mash maybe a stone of potatoes, probably Kerr Pinks, with boiling milk, a good dollop of butter, and a handful of chopped parsley. They'd beat the lot to a pure white fluffiness flecked with bright green.

Spooned out on a hot plate for each of us, a hole quickly forked in the middle, melted butter poured in, and a poached egg on top, the mash was our dinner. If it was fattening, well, we were young and we were growing. Mother knew her potatoes. Kerr Pinks were for mashing or for roasting in their jackets. The firm creamy Records she liked for slicing and quick roasting with bacon fat in the top of a hot oven to be served with mealied herrings or mackerel. Records were good for potato salad. They kept their shape the best and had a nice texture for eating cold. She cut a deep cross on Queens, inserted a thin strip of bacon and roasted them. We were given them with a slice of pork liver, fried in

Basil, me, Joe, Mena, Kevin and Phauds

whatever fat was to hand, and carrots cooked with onion and a couple of cloves for flavour.

Golden Wonders were special and expensive. They bridged the gap between winter and spring, between the end of the old potatoes and the beginning of the new. New potatoes were always boiled in their jackets with some sprigs of mint and served as a separate course with plenty of butter and fresh sprigs of mint for decoration. With a glass of fresh buttermilk they were reckoned to be as good a dinner as you'd get in whatever *haute cuisine* establishment struck Mother's fancy at the time. Left-over mash with leeks and milk and little bits of bacon through it made soup. Or potato cakes with sausages and fried apple rings for tea. Or fish cakes with egg and finnan haddie or smoked cod. It goes without saying there was no waste!

Bridget made the bread. Other girls came and went but Bridget was constant, one of the family, and, I think, mother's best friend. She took no cheek from any of us and mother backed her up when she told us to mind our manners or made us tidy up after ourselves. She bloomed in the heat of the kitchen and graced it in her flowered blouse, her full, long, blue woollen skirt and white apron. From her hair, pinned high in a bun on the back of her head, to her shining patent-toed shoes she was as neat and clean as they're made.

Never was Bridget's labour more appreciated or its fruit more enjoyed than when the fire in the range glowed redly and a warm crusty smell grew tangible in delicious taste. Brown bread, or wheaten bread, as we called it, was an everyday affair. Bridget had a 'wee bowl' about the size of a breakfast cup. It held 'a wee bit more than a fistful' she explained. Her proportions were one bowl of flour to two bowls of wholemeal, a half teaspoon of salt, a whole one of sugar and a level one of baking soda which was all the sodium bicarbonate we ever needed for indigestion was unknown.

She turned the soda for all her bread-making into the palm of her left hand, crushed the lumps with the back of a spoon, and scraped it into the basin on top of the other ingredients. Her fingers worked to a definite rhythm as she mixed the dry stuff, caught it up in her fingers, and let it fall again, aerated and evenly mixed. She would then look around for her wooden spoon. It would almost certainly have been 'fiddled' with and, threatening to 'give a good skelp' to the culprit, she would take it gently enough, and with two quick movements, make a well in the centre.

The spoon poised to stir in her right hand, with her left she would give the milk in the jug a 'birl' or two before pouring it into the well. She never misjudged the amount. The dough was never too wet or too dry, but left the bowl clean as she turned it out on the floured board. She made kneading an art, so lightly and deftly she did it. Finally, cutting a cross on the top with a wet knife to bless the work and to prevent cracks, she would put the nicely shaped oval on to a greased baking tin and into a moderate oven for about an hour. A dollop of bacon or chicken dripping on top when the cake was nearly cooked gave it a special savoury flavour.

Thrift was her second nature. If the oven was ever hot for any purpose Bridget never neglected to put in 'a bit o' soda bread.' Cake we never got or missed. On high days, two thin layers of soda dough with chopped sour apple, sugar and a clove or two in between, the edges pressed all round between finger and thumb and cooked, made apple bread a real treat. When Bridget had the patience or mother the time, one or other would butter the upper crust, sprinkle coarse sugar over and put it back in the oven to become crunchy-topped. A piece of cheese along with it and there was a meal which took no coaxing to eat.

Currant bread was always 'curranty' whether the fruit was currants, sultanas or raisins; but to wash the fruit and mix it into the soda-bread ingredients was not enough for us. A crossed bones and skull, an initial or a name, or a cat, had to pattern the top in fruit before the cake went into the oven. Nothing kept us so quiet or so contented than a bit of dough each, to knead and roll and stretch and pull and stud with a dropped currant or two looking like so many dirty little bits of putty, and to have them placed in the oven. But dirty and misshapen and all as they were, dare any one of us commit a mistake in identity! They were happily eaten and points compared.

Seedy bread, though not so popular, was made by simply adding a dessert spoon of caraway or cummin seeds to the dry ingredients for soda bread. It was considered good for windy people and perhaps for this reason the old people liked it. It was better a day or so old, for by then the seedy flavour had spread and of all ways to eat it the best was fried with sausages for breakfast.

Treacle bread to us was what the world called ginger cake. It was made every Friday. Mother maintained that it kept us 'right' and indeed the weekly dose was unknown in our house. The treacle, or molasses, was fetched by the pound from the chemist or grocer. The jar was set in a pan of hot water to make its contents runny. The dry ingredients were prepared as for soda bread with a large teaspoon of cinnamon and of ground ginger, a heaped ta-

With Joe and kittens

blespoon of brown sugar, and a generous knob of butter rubbed in. A handful of sultanas and some chopped crystallised ginger were occasional extras. Two large tablespoonfuls of treacle to four bowls of flour were Bridget's proportions. All her baking was done to scolding of the boys, singing to the baby and instructions to the girls. The crumbs were awarded to 'the best' and the lick of the treacly spoon was always given to the one who had fetched the treacle and I never remember the award made without a subsequent fight for possession.

Griddle bread, made from Indian corn meal or 'yalla male', as Coalisland called it, many a time soothed that cross half-hour before bed-time which all young families know. The finest 'yalla male' was known as Golden Drop and we all knew what Bridget meant when she said: 'Scald m'wee bowl o' Golden Drop for me there.'

The oldest one present, Molly or Nina, would empty the meal into a basin and pour just enough boiling water over it to cause it to swell without making it wet. Bridget had mixed two bowls of white flour, a spot of sugar, a pinch of salt and a half-teaspoon of bread soda in her mixing bowl. When the meal had cooled a little she blended them all together with just enough buttermilk to make a firm dough. This was floured and rolled out in a thin flat round, then dextrously transferred to the heated and lightly greased griddle.

The moment for turning the thin round cake was high adventure to us and we glowed with joy when the feat was achieved for Indian bread is inclined to crack and be crumbly. The time to turn it was guessed by the rise and the undercrust and was achieved by firmly taking the furthest edge by fingers and thumbs, sliding it almost off the edge of the griddle, up, and over. Ah! loving memory of it, hot off the griddle and elbowing fight for the long thin middle slice, its lovely golden glow shining through butter near to melting.

Every baking day was a hey-day. Our shiny brown crock, of the kind used for well water, was used for buttermilk in our house. Every drop of sweet and sour milk that might otherwise be wasted went into it for every pint of buttermilk meant a cake of bread and every cake was different. To be allowed to lift the wooden lid off the crock, to cut up the solid inch-deep top of the milk with a scalded knife, to plunge in a bellied jug and to watch the little floes plop over the rim was reward indeed for five minutes bursting quiet in the kitchen when Bridget warned we'd give her a sore head if we didn't 'give over'.

Churning was elementary. It consisted of decanting the milk briskly and often from one vessel to another until it foamed. The favour of 'raising the milk' was granted to the older children in turn except when, fairly frequently Bridget would shout us out with 'G'on outa that from undther m'feet or ah'll never get done the day.' She never did get done that day, nor any other day while her life lasted. She was one of those who worked for love and, not only that, but she sang as she did it.

Drama took over at Hallowe'en. The companionable 'blop' of a huge apple dumpling, simmering away on the stove all day, preceded the ritual for which we waited with fearful hope that the miracle would occur. We sat round the kitchen table, napkins and spoons in hands, and waited. No plate was big enough so a meat dish, with carving knife and serving spoon at either end, lay ready. Milk, infused for an hour or so with a couple of bay leaves, was being made into a thin sweet sauce with cornflour and sugar to be poured into jugs and passed around.

At last, a few sharp exchanges of 'You'll scald yourself,' 'Hand that cloth,' 'Easy now. Easy,' announced the imminence of the revelation. Bridget carried the dumpling in its bowl to the table on the baking board. The meat dish was inverted over its pallid cap. Between them, Mother and Bridget managed to turn them over. Bridget removed the board. Mother looked hard at the bottom of the upturned bowl as if to defy its contents to fail her. Then, holding the bowl with a cloth, she slowly, slowly, slipped it off the standing pudding. She lifted the carving knife and serving spoon and looked around the table at our expectant faces.

With quick decision, she plunged the knife into the dumpling's crown and drew it to its base. A second's delay and then a thick ooze of blood-red juice and apple stretched the cut and stained the fleshy dough. Little Joe and I banged the table and cheered with the rest although we hardly knew what the fuss was about and didn't really like the mess on our plates; but we loved the sweet sauce and were given as much as we wanted of that. That white apple should become deep red was a mystery. Mother was a magician! Joe was convinced she could do anything at all she wanted to do.

Miss Hiss

Joe was an odd wee thing. He never strayed far from the kitchen where he'd sit for hours on the cross bar under the big table. 'Where's my wee magpie?' Bridget would call out to him when she felt like being sociable. Out would peep the big grey eyes through the thick red fringe. He'd grin up at her, ingratiating. He always seemed to have a tooth missing and I suppose it was that, and his funny squashed nose, that made everybody make such a pet of him.

Bridget favoured him over the rest of us though she'd never admit it; but it was always he who would get the lick of a pot or a spoon when she'd tell us we should be ashamed of ourselves for asking. But then, he didn't annoy her the way we did. What he liked to do, above all, as he sat under the table, was to make dolls. He'd make dolls from anything, from candle grease to a wooden spoon and you wouldn't believe the neat way he'd turn any old scrap of cloth into a skirt or a shirt or a pair of pants. His pockets were always stuffed with bright bits he'd pick up when an older sister cut out a dress or made a patchwork cushion for the school bazaar.

One winter, when he was about five he began making clothes for Miss Hiss. That was his name for her. Miss Hiss. She was the goose Bridget was fattening for the Christmas dinner. 'That oul goose,' she'd say,''ll have us atin' out of house an' home. Gon' out, pet, an' throw her a few scraps—an'thin' to keep her away from that back door.' It may have been cupboard love on Miss Hiss' part but, anyway, she and Joe got very attached and she didn't mind a bit when he'd dress her up in a bonnet or shawl he'd made for her. He'd stand back and admire her waddling around the yard and then he'd waddle after to adjust the set of whatever creation she was wearing at the time.

Mother had gone to Belfast for the day and we were agog for her to come home for we knew she'd be loaded with mysterious parcels for Christmas. There was a job had to be done when she was away and Bridget had the doing of it. No doubt that was why she was so bad tempered all the morning and why she threw us all out of the kitchen after dinner-time, even Joe. She'd had to mind him all day to keep him from feeding the goose. He couldn't understand why poor Miss Hiss had to be starved so he was very down in himself.

We missed him around four when the light began to fail and we gathered into the kitchen out of the cold. 'Where's Joe?' Bridget asked. We looked at each other. None of us knew where he was. He wasn't under the table. He wasn't upstairs. Lord! The panic! Calling. Shouting his name. Bridget was frantic. She sent for the men in Devlin's pub and got them to comb the brick yard. It was full of holes. It was a mercy none of them fell into one considering the day that was in it. They whistled and hallooed all over the place but there was no sign of Joe.

Bridget commanded us to stay in the kitchen, not to move, as she went from door to window. We whimpered, too frightened to cry. Bridget was white-faced and tight-lipped, trying to control herself. She told us that the priest, the police and the men would surely find him. 'Pray God he's found before your poor mother comes home. But I can't face killin' that goose the day. She'll have to be fed. Get the lantern one of' ye, till ah see t'er.'

In the shed Mena held the lantern high for Bridget to see by and there they were, the pair of them, deep and snug in the warm straw. He was fast asleep, curled up beside her. She reared and glared with vicious hungry eyes, stretched her long neck and hissed with fury at the light. You'll understand why we had no goose for dinner that Christmas and why we've never had the heart to eat goose since.

The Twelfth

On the twelfth of July the town was taken over for the day by the Orange Brethren. With bands and banners in a noisy, colourful, exuberant display they renewed undying loyalty to a long dead king. The Ancient Order of Hibernians had their procession on the 17th of March to celebrate our conversion to Christianity by St Patrick. The Orange procession was better than the Hibernians'; it was longer, wilder and much, much louder. Every townland sent its band and supporters and every band played party tunes with all its might. On long nights before the big day, and into the small hours, we'd lie awake listening with fearful delight to the Killyman Wreckers practising. The sound they made had a terrible relentless rhythm as the sticks thwacked the tight skins of the enormous drums. It was said that after the practice the drummers' wrists were torn and bleeding and we believed it.

The 12th of July was a bonus for us, a sort of extra Christmas. We had to stay in the house all day 'for fear of trouble' and because of that my mother made a party of it. She herself wouldn't be seen watching the procession but we hung out of the windows in Bridget's charge, as familiar faces, grimly self-conscious under hard black hats, went bobbing past. Bridget talked to herself, hardly able to contain her excitement:

'God a' God, wud ye luk at oul' McCracken. That's the sash his father wore, all right. Sure, it's thrippin' 'im. That cudn't be wee Corley that turned to marry Houston's daughter? That wee fella wi' the buttoned boots? The cut of 'im! Och, dear oh dear. There's the minister. Susie Kelly o'Limavady made that apron he's wearin'. God forgive her. Wudn't ye think, now, that Ballygawley cud get a matchin' pair to carry the banner? Lukitit, all down one side wi' John Wilson's short leg."

We only half heard her for the endless procession of lodges, bands and banners' bearers was made up of dream people; not the men who pulled teeth or killed the pigs or lived mysterious lives in London most of the year. The banners depicting the Battle of the Boyne were huge oil paintings. It took great skill to balance them which was why the men holding the poles danced along and staggered against the breeze in order to keep them aloft. Bridget explained that they weren't drunk.

'Aye, but ah wudn't answer for the night,' she scorned and looked blacker than any Orangeman.

The Killyman Wreckers transfixed us when they came into view. Everyone knew that if they caught a Catholic they'd beat him into mince-meat and eat him raw. And it's true that when some dignitaries from the South spent a night in a hotel in the Moy, the Wreckers practised all night under their bedroom windows and tore their nerves to shreds. Their drums were held by wide leather straps crossed over their shoulders and balanced on their thrusting stomachs. The drummers wore bowler hats and orange sashes over white shirts, the sleeves in arm-bands. They seemed to walk in a trance, drawn on by the drums, drugged by their own hypnotic hail-storm of noise. We watched the drum-sticks striking like knives and thought, with scary thrills, of mince-meat.

We understood that the procession was in honour of King William of Glorious and Immortal Memory, whoever he was, but Bridget dinned it into us that Glorious Saint Patrick, dear saint of our Isle, was the true patron of Ireland. 'It doesn't matter anyway,' she said, 'Good people'll all end up t'gether, high in his mansions above, whether they want to or not, when they die, so mind an' behave yerselves or ye might end up like Bob William's oul' Orange flute an' burn in hell for all eternity.' Bridget never spared us the terror of her beliefs.

The soldier

A soldier called at the house one afternoon. He was looking for my brother Daniel who, he said, had been in his class at school. As it happened, Daniel had gone with Father to Aughnacloy.

Mother wasn't too sure when they would be back but she asked him in to wait. He was very shy and looked a bit stiff in his khaki uniform and brown boots. Mother got him to repeat his name. Ted McNeilis. Not MacNeill. She said it wasn't a very common name, not one you'd easily forget. She knew a girl once, a Teeny Murray, married a McNeilis. Tyrone. They were both from Tyrone. 'She's my mother.' The soldier smiled a big happy smile.

He relaxed and settled down to the plate of bacon and eggs, with brown bread and tea that she set before him. She apologised that our dinner was over 'But sure that'll keep you going for a while,' she said. She told him that it would be quite all right to undo the neck button of his tunic for comfort and if he cared to loosen the laces of his boots to rest his feet there'd be no harm in that either. Mena and Joe and I were enchanted. A soldier!

'Did you ever shoot a body down dead?' Joe asked him.

'I did not and I hope I never have to, but if you like I'll tell you about a battle long ago when men were shot dead and for no good reason. Would you like that?' Ted asked.

'We would, we would,' we told him urgently.

He began by reciting the beginning of a ballad which, he said, had been written to commemorate the Battle of Black Bridge.

> Old Tyrone—first in the field and last to leave!
> Glorious Clonoe will plant the tree of liberty. . .
> That our posterity may say when mourning o'er our
>   graves
> Those heroes died for liberty rather than live like slaves.

'The Black Bridge was in the place called Clonoe. It was Cluain Oig in the old days when the people spoke Irish. It means Holy Meadow and it was holy because a penal Mass stone was hidden away in the trees on one of the banks rising from the river. At that time it was against the law to say Mass, and it was against the law to attend, so the priest and the people had to make their own arrangements in secret and hope to get away with it.'

'What happened if they got caught?'

'Aw, now, they'd have a hard time of it, I'm telling you. Anyhow, the people depended on the Black Bridge if they had to cross the river from one side to the other to make a quick getaway. It was near enough to Clonoe Chapel and the Mass Stone was not much further on.

'Well, on the Twelfth of July in 1829 word came that the Orangemen were on the march with the intention of destroying the chapel. A call went out in double quick time to the men of Clonoe to come and defend it. The way I heard it was that three tall Corrs from Rosehill led them. The women fell in as well. They carried armsful of flannel and rags for to push powder and ammunition in the blunderbusses and muskets the men were carrying.'

Blunderbusses and muskets! Joe was mesmerised.

'It wasn't just the women,' Ted went on. 'The children ran to pick up big stones and dropped them into the women's gathered-up aprons. They spoke no word. They sang no song. However they managed it, they kept the Orangemen at bay. Towards evening the attackers decided to parley. The Catholic leader, Hugh O'Neill, held up a white cloth and walked to the middle of the bridge but he was dropped by a treacherous shot. His father, John O'Neill ran to him, but he was shot and killed as well. The Clonoe men and women were raging. Furious. Two more of their men were killed but a Fenian bullet, as the ballad tells us, "felled the Orange leader from off his horse!"

'The attackers flew in disorder before a fresh charge from the men of Clonoe and a savage volley of stones from the women. The next day the district was quiet while Clonoe prepared to bury its dead. Nobody thought for a minute that the Orangemen would be up to anything but, in fact, a few of them sneaked back and set fire to the chapel. A decent Protestant neighbour raised the alarm and the fire was put out before the chapel was destroyed altogether.'

'Did anybody get burned?' Mena asked hopefully.

'Nobody did,' said Ted. 'The chapel's still there, you know.' Over a hundred years later the parish priest of Clonoe, a Father Clarke, took it in hand. He got the charred beams and rafters turned into pedestals for statues and the charred places covered with glass in memory of the people who saved the chapel all those years ago.

'You'd let me talk here till midnight,' Ted said as he bent to tie his boot laces. 'I have to go. Tell Daniel I was asking for him. Tell him never to forget old Tyrone.' He shook hands with Mother and thanked her for the tea. And then he saluted. Joe saluted everyone in sight for days afterwards.

The hotel

Peter McAleer owned the hotel which is to say that he owned a whole world. Its front was nothing much to look at—two rows of five windows across at the top and two windows on each side of the door, all veiled by white lace curtains. The heavy front door opened, and it was always open, into a bare tiled porch. The name of a previous owner, MONTAGUE'S HOTEL, was engraved in a horse-shoe shape in frosted glass on the upper panel of the inner door.

Peter McAleer was as decent a man as you'd meet on a day's march. I was always a little afraid of him. He seemed to live his life in a state of indignation, his pale blue eyes popping out of his head and his grizzled hair always ruffled. He was hotelier, barman, auctioneer, undertaker, estate agent, farmer, and he had a heart as big as a house. It was he who buried the poor for nothing, paid for an ailing woman's holiday, bailed the town drunkard out of jail and was always good for tuppence for the pictures on a Saturday.

It was in his traps that we trotted the townlands with his yardmen posting bills for forthcoming sales. It was on his drays that we heavened home from the hay field on summer evenings, drowsed with the scent of tickling grasses and glimpsing sky through high branches of trees along the Donoughmore road.

The McAleer children called their mother Mama and so did we. She was tall, calm. She had presence. She moved at a pace never less than stately. She carried the keys of the kitchen store-room but sometimes forgot to remove them from the keyhole when she went upstairs for her habitual afternoon rest. Edie would take the opportunity to abstract a couple of packets of Jacob's Cream Crackers and invite us to share them down the yard in the hay-shed. That they were stolen goods never cost us a thought.

She let us play in the old disused kitchens in the basement. It was as good a way as any of keeping the young McAleers and their friends away from the business part of the hotel. The basement kitchen, by the time we knew it, had given way to another altogether more practical power-house on the ground floor, to be the centre of the catering, laundering and general domestic needs of the hotel. The basement was called the low kitchen and it hoarded treasure.

There were iron lasts of all sizes for the mending of boots and shoes and wooden lasts to keep shoes and riding boots in shape. Goffering irons and box irons hinted at upstairs elegance. Big copper preserving pans had jelly moulds, stone hot-water bottles, utensils of unimaginable use, thrown into them. Two copper fish kettles were big enough to hold the most mystical of salmon. Stone crocks, glazed brown and yellow and black, rested on the tops of a couple of old dressers which were hung with cracked mugs and jugs. Old country furniture, out of date but beautifully made, waited in safety for rediscovery. Three-legged stools, flow-ery spittoons, chamber pots and wash-stand basins with match-ing jugs, holding every size of wooden spoon and ladle, had found refuge on big scrubbed pine tables. Rid of their jetsam and pushed together, the tables made an ideal stage.

We played for hours down there, at 'house' or in improvised plays. So many props to hand prompted scenes for their use. We had only to think of Mrs S., who lay on her sofa all day gently coughing her life away; who kept her daughters by her to brush her long dark hair; to dab her forehead with vinegar and water; to open the door to the doctor who asked her to open her mouth and say 'Aaah' and took her temperature. It was easy to greet her sailor husband, back from some faraway place and to tell him, tearfully, that he was just in time. Sometimes she died and sometimes she recovered as when 'Father' produced from his pocket a sachet of powder ground from the roots of rare plants, given to him by pygmies he had rescued from gorillas in the rain-forest.

The plots depended on the number of players, who wandered in and out of the action as the fancy took them. Between the McAleers and us, the yardman's beautiful daughter, Alice, and a favoured few from school, we could always get up a play or a concert. Concerts allowed everyone to play a part for everyone had a talent for something; singing, reciting or dancing, solo or duet or all together. We tried out Miss Hennessy's set dances. Miss Hennessy was the school dancing mistress. She was from Cork and she did her best to instil into us a love of our native culture. 'Arrah,' she'd cry, 'When I come here to teach ye can't ye lift yer legs t'larn. Arrah, one two three four five six seven, arrah one two three . . . '

She was abetted by Sister Brigid who came from Dublin. The educational system did not encourage inclusion of the Irish language, but Sister Brigid defied it. She taught us prayers, the Our Father, the Hail Mary, and the Glory Be in Irish and a short dialogue, a polite exchange between neighbours, which we learned by heart so that we could run it off without pause if with only a vague understanding of the words. It was on Sister Brigid's and Miss Hennessy's account that, down in the low kitchen, we belted out rebel songs in support of the boys who thought of themselves as red hot republicans.

There was always some entertaining activity going on in McAleer's yard. The kitchen was the first of the workrooms that strung out all the way down to the hay-shed at the very end. His dairy, next the kitchen, held the wide shallow pans of milk, clotting for churning. If churning was going on we might be allowed a few dashes with the plunger which pierced the lid of the lovely waisted wooden churn in the middle of the tiled kitchen floor and would be given a drink of delicious buttermilk when the dashing was done and the butter gathered into a scalded wooden bowl.

A bottling machine beside the bar door jammed steaming hot corks into the necks of beer and porter bottles, a job that couldn't possibly be done by fingers. We watched horses being shod and wrinkled our noses at the pungent smell of burning horn as the blacksmith drove nails through holes in hot iron shoes to secure them to the hooves of patient uncomplaining animals. We might even get a turn at the handle of the turnip-cutting machine making feed for the farm animals. We had parties in the hay-shed. The sun came through a small square window under the roof. Iridescent motes danced a mad fandango in its rays as we slid from one level to another. We drank lemonade and ate Paris buns on the highest level and lay in a dream listening to the seductive cooing and the soft whirr of feathers as pigeons swooped and settled.

The boys thought it funny sometimes to put out a hand for a piece of a bun and to release a tiny field mouse, petrified with fear by our screams. But down in the empty open shed, where carts and traps were parked on market day, the best drama of all was played on the day the pig was killed. We jostled for places on the mossy wall opposite the cemented killing ground, the girls as keen as the boys to secure a good view. We cheered to high heaven when Kelly, the yardman, drove the bright blue-painted cart into the yard, let down the ramp and prodded the pig into a tumbling frightened trot away from its prison.

We held our breath as Mena prepared to respond to the dare of one or other of our brothers. Slowly, she eased herself off the wall and made for the animal that had placed itself into a corner of the shed as if to hide in black oblivion. It shuddered when it felt her weight on its back and took off around the yard in a rolling waddle trying to dislodge its rider as she half rode, half pedalled it, while we clung to each other in hysterical laughter and cheered them on until Kelly and his helper, McCusker, arrived with huge kettles of boiling water and a bundle of bamboo sticks.

Kelly grabbed my sister by a fistful of the back of her jersey and jerked her off the animal's back as they lolloped past. He roared at her to 'Go home and behave yerself ye bold wee brat ye' but she ran to the wall and hoisted herself to a choice position.

Poor pig. A ferocious blow to the side of the head with a wooden mallet knocked it out. How the white enamel buckets got filled with blood and entrails I never knew for I couldn't bear to look. We were silent in the moment it took to turn pig into pork and in the silence we knew that something momentous had happened. When someone nudged me and muttered 'He's dead. You can look now,' I opened my eyes to see the poor fellow slit all the way down the front and Kelly slowly pouring boiling water over him while McCusker scraped off the top skin and hair with a long knife leaving him lovely and clean and pink.

After that the men opened him wide and kept him stretched with bamboo sticks cut to the width of the carcass. They put butcher's hooks through his trotters and hung him upside down from a beam in the roof. I was sure his little eyes blinked when they threw clean water over him and left him to drip. Wee Joe, the youngest there, was mournful. 'He's not a bit like the pig any more,' he said, and you could see he was grieving.

It was all over except for the boys' scramble for the bladder. It would have to be cleaned and scraped and rinsed and blown up and tied before they could call it a football. One of the girls might be given the liver to take home. It must have come to our house once for I remember it, parboiled, sitting on a dish near the frying-pan when anyone could cut off a slice and fry it in the bacon fat of the breakfast rashers. I never could eat a bit of it, though, thinking of those white-lashed blinking eyes.

Soulful and sorry

The hotel's commercial room was private for the day to the women who came into the town for the market. Their orders of small ports produced port of a peculiar colour for the colour staining the glass was a pale straw and not the rich and purply red one would expect to see. For some reason port was a respectable drink for women and whiskey was not. Whiskey was a man's drink.

The women sat in groups of threes and fours, backs to doors and windows, talking in whispers, slowing and flowing in confidential rushes and short knowing exchanges. At the opening of a door or the shadow of a form at a window, the heads suspended animation. The eyes, in a sidelong glance, would fix the intruder, a child or a man or a stranger. They'd will it to back out and go in a flutter of muttered apologies.

The yardmen watered and fed their men's horses and minded traps, brakes and carts. By now, after years in the place, they'd know every owner as much by his habits as by his name and could judge, just nicely, how far it was safe to back McEndoo's trap between the shafts of Kelly's cart and whether or not the brake for the mill would be away in time to let Carbery out with his clattery old side-car. Around six in the evening the exodus would begin.

A 'Get in, woman, get in,' a 'Hurry up man, for goodness sake, will ye, if we're to get home the night,' a last check of bought provisions, a jingle of harness and a 'Hup there' to the horses hurried them all for home. Plug tobacco was sure to have been bought but some favoured a certain brand which was already flaked. It came in a flat round tin, packed in waxed white paper neatly pleated in to the centre with a white pipe cleaner curled on top. The cleaner looked like a worm and it, and the pleated paper, always reminded me of the fun we had playing in the coffin house when all the people had gone.

The smell was a clean compound of pinewood, resin, size and tar. Coffins in all sizes and stages of preparation leaned against the walls and sometimes there was one on trestles being finished in a hurry. The padding was a work of art, a smooth upholstery job of layer upon layer of brown wadding covered with fine white linen tightly tacked in place and trimmed with yards of goffered linen expertly glued round the edge.

We fought for possession of the odd quarter-yard or so that might be left on the reel to give a romantic burial to anything dead, from a drowned kitten to a scythed field mouse; but our favourite game was playing dead. We easily slid into a state of heartfelt sympathy or hopeless grief according to which of us lay still with closed eyes and clasped hands in an unfinished coffin chosen for size; but the coffin-man soon tired of our game and our questions and chased us.

'Who's dead?' we'd ask.

'Oul Carson down the Donaghmore Road,' he might say.

'What happened him?'

'He fell over a straw and a hen kicked him.'

'Was he very old?' we'd persist.

'As oul as yer granny', he'd shout vindictively. 'Gon away t'yer beds now, the whole o' ye or ah'll nail ye down,' and home we'd go.

If none of the elderly farmers who came into the market square on market day suggested a model for oul Carson, framed in goffered linen in his pine-wood coffin, we looked at each other in speculation when once in a while the coffin-man worked at a job so small that we could hardly see, from behind his back, what he was at. But we could guess and, sooner or later, from pride, he'd let us in to see his handiwork—the shaped and white-painted box, the satin lining and the special lacy edging for infants. The way he handled it put us in mind of a cradle.

We saw one, once, being wedged into a trap with a big basket of groceries to hold it in position. Tears streamed down the face of the man who drove it away. Even we were too stricken by awe to make any remark, but the man and his load and its mystery left a query of wonder in our minds. For a man to cry like that!

I longed to die. I would look so beautiful, like a doll in a fancy box. After the funeral I would swoop and soar over the heads of all my friends and relations. They would look up and wave to me as I spiralled away, high over the tops of the cemetery trees, away, away up to heaven. It never occurred to me that I might be barred from heaven for the time, at evening devotions, I called out loudly, in a rush, for all the congregation to hear 'pray for us, pray for us' in an effort to hurry the Dean who bored everyone the way he dragged out the litany of the saints.

When Tina, the baby sister of a girl in my class did die, I mitched from school to go and see her. Out of respect I turned my pinny inside out for Bridget refused to give me a clean one, it being near the end of the week. I polished the toes of my shoes on the back of my black-stockinged legs. I felt a bit daunted when I entered the door of the little two-roomed house in Shamble Lane. On the way I'd imagined just me, admiring and soulful and sorry, and Tina putting the finishing touches to the coffin-man's work. The room was full of women. They buzzed and nudged each other but I paid little attention to them after the first shock.

The candles that burned on the window-sill drew me to the little coffin resting in a bright hedge of flowers on chairs around it. There were roses framing the tiny pale blue face on the little pillow and a pink glass rosary twined the bleached twigs of Tina's fingers. I knelt down but quickly got up again because, kneeling, I couldn't see Tina. I thought I should cry, but I couldn't. No one was crying. Not even the mother. She sat near Tina's head and she looked more pleased than anything, I suppose because the child looked so nice.

She laughed with the other women when my sister suddenly came in and grabbed my arm.

'You're to come at once', she said grimly, 'You're going to be killed.'

I pulled away from her and had time to tear my blue bow out of my hair and to plank it on the baby's head before getting a thump on the back which sent me through the door. I didn't care who had betrayed me. I had seen Tina and, after school, I would tell the coffin-man how she looked in her wee white cot, sleeping, and not crying any more.

Nuns and notions

It was common practice for the Catholic young of the town to start their education as 'low babies' at the convent school. They began their formal learning making numbers and letters with their fingers in trays of sand. 'High babies' progressed to slates. Slate pencils screeched out 'cat', 'sat', 'mat', until they conquered the sentence 'The cat sat on the mat.' They were promoted to pencil and paper and Vere Foster's headlines to copy when the time came to practice 'a good hand'. But there was more to education than book-learning.

We had to take turns at providing frog-spawn for nature study. We put it in water in jam jars and placed them on the window-sill for everyone to see the spawn turn into tadpoles. We never saw the change for it was spawn one day, tadpoles the next. They were thrown out when they started to eat each other, but certainly they never became frogs. On Fridays we were given small pieces of beeswax and rags and told to give our desks a good polish. The wax had a holy sort of smell, very pleasant, but it resisted contact with the wood and stuck in thickish smears as we tried to spread it with the rag.

Nancy Mullin had the brilliant idea of bringing in her own rag steeped in turpentine in a used cocoa tin but there was such a build-up of wax that the rag dragged obstinate streaks along the desk lid and it took an awful lot of rubbing to get an even glow. Soon we had all wheedled a ready-mix of wax and turpentine from our mothers and enjoyed the competition of getting the best shine.

As time went on and we grew older membership of the Children of Mary was awarded to girls whom the nuns perceived to be 'good.' The insignia was a medal depicting Our Lady Queen of Heaven, sewn to a necklace of pale blue ribbon. As I never received it I never knew what was expected of the Children of Mary apart from their care of the altar which dominated the classroom. I left my place in class one day and sat in beside Nancy because Sister Brigid had slapped her and she was crying. I put my arm around her shoulder. When Sister ordered me back to my place I stuck out my tongue at her. I was not good.

Even so, I walked the convent grounds in the May procession. I *felt* good singing loudly,

> An angel of mercy
> Led Bernadette's feet
> Where flows the great torrent
> Our Lady to-oo greet
> Ave, ave, ave Maree-eea
> Ave, ave, ave Maree-eea.

I wondered why the great torrent wanted to greet Our Lady and if Bernadette got her feet wet. The bluebells we held, so bright and crisp when we started, soon lolled dejectedly in our hands. By the time we were half-way round the grounds I was wondering what 'Ave' meant. A brother told me that it meant 'Hello' which I thought to be a lot friendlier than 'Ave' but no one would sing it with me when we sang the hymn again after prayers in the classroom.

The nuns dressed in many-pleated skirts of black serge, deep, starched white bibs, waist length veils, black for the fully professed, white for novices, and white starched linen caps, stretched across their foreheads and tied at the back under the veils. In spite of this attempt at anonymity the differences between the nuns were plain to see for they were of all sorts, tall, short, fat, thin, young and old, kind or cross. The order and its rules made no difference to their personalities. Even if they tried to change when they 'entered', even if they tried to leave the world behind them as they were supposed to do, the world stayed close to their heels.

Mother Borgia taught us English. She was also the convent gardener. She was small and round and had a face, someone said, like a crab-apple. It was certainly red-cheeked and a little withered. She seemed to resent having to leave the garden for she always came into class in a rush, still with her heavy outer skirt hooked up to the waist of her equally heavy underskirt and wearing her muddy boots.

'Read that,' she would say brusquely to one of us, pointing with an earth-encrusted finger-nail to a passage in a Shakespearian play.

'Stomach, child, stomach!' she furiously censored when the child read 'In fair round belly with good capon lined,' from *As You Like it*. The rest of the class tittered. They laughed outright when I, tired of the timorous reading from *Hamlet*, declaimed 'To be, or not to be? *That* is the question' with a violent slash at the air with my forefinger.

'Quiet!' Mother Borgia roared. Then: 'Carry on you,' she ordered, glaring at Marie Farrell beside me who mumbled a few lines before giving way to the next girl who, in turn, deferred to her neighbour until the class ended to our headlong relief.

We invented fantasies about the nuns. Sister Brigid had been very beautiful when she was young. She took the veil when the man she loved and was to marry was killed while performing a heroic deed, any heroic deed, in a foreign land during a war. When she was cross, we decided, it was because she was lonely and unhappy; but she always made up for a bad mood by letting us sing a Tom Moore melody together towards the end of our lesson in arithmetic. A melody, especially 'She Is Far From the Land', made us feel sad and happy at the same time and that was how Sister looked when we sang.

She and Mother Borgia passed each other by without a look or a word. We heard that Sister Brigid had asked Reverend Mother for permission to suggest to 'the gardener' that she might grow asparagus and tomatoes as well as potatoes and cabbages. Mother Borgia was mortally offended at being called 'the gardener' and never spoke to Sister Brigid again. It was a bad business because Borgia did, in fact, begin to grow asparagus and tomatoes and other things such as French beans just to show what she could do if she wanted to. She insisted, though, that giving them to the nuns would only give them notions and, except for the odd treat for Reverend Mother and her visitors, they went to Canon Quinn.

Sister Josephine must be the daughter of a lord, we dreamed, for she had such dainty ways and such long white fingers. Even when she turned back her sleeves to show us how to roll out pastry, in domestic economy, she did it as if it was made of such precious stuff that it had to be touched with the finger-tips only and very lightly at that. She taught us deportment too.

Chins up. Shoulders back. Arms hanging loosely by the sides. No folding across the chest. Sit straight. Do NOT SLOUCH. Never, NEVER cross the knees. Ankles only. No running except in play. Speak quietly and clearly. She taught us the walk of a queen, each with a book balanced on her head. Sister Josephine was very hard to please but we enjoyed her lessons for they gave us a chance to act at being ladies. She reproved us when she had to by tapping us in the middle of the forehead with the blunt end of a pencil to the rhythm of 'Giddy little Miss. Giddy little Miss' until the message reached our giddy little brains.

Then there was pale, despairing Sister Pauline who distributed paper, pencils, broken crayons, baldy brushes, stubs of pastels and rations of powder paint to us. She drew a flower or a bird or a tree on the blackboard and told us to copy it although we had only to look out the window to see them in reality. She must have known that she could not teach us to draw movement and that we were not ready to learn. Mostly she sat at her desk reading but now and again she would creep around, look over a shoulder, murmur 'Good. Good,' take a crayon from a hand and make a listless mark.

Sometimes she brought a book for us to look at; to introduce us to the work of famous artists, she said, whose original paintings we might one day see if we were lucky. In spasms of wan enthusiasm she might tell us a story about one of these masters. Such a one was a boy who minded sheep somewhere in the hills in Italy. He loved to draw pictures with a stone on the rocks. A true artist is never deterred from following his vocation for want of brush and paint, she told us, and we thought it strange of her to call art a vocation as we knew that only nuns and priests had vocations and that they were 'called' by God to follow Him.

Anyhow, this country nobody got his heart's desire and was invited to work at the studio of an artist in Florence. His great talent was nurtured, Sister Pauline said, by his patron. A duke was sent by the King to bring to him samples of the best paintings of the best artists in the country as he wanted to commission only the best for the decoration of his palace. The young artist drew a perfect circle at one go. The duke was offended but the artist insisted that he give it to the king. 'He will understand,' he said. The King did understand and that shepherd boy became one of the greatest and most influential artists in the history of European art. His name was Giotto.

Sister Pauline was out of herself when she told this story and you could see by the faraway look in her eyes that she believed it and that she would have loved to have been like him if only she had had a different vocation. She had no vocation for sewing but she had to teach it to us. We each worked on a piece of white lawn called 'a specimen.' By the time it was hemmed, running-stitched, back-stitched, top-stitched, run-and-fell seamed, herring-boned, button-holed, tucked and honey-combed it was grubby and blood-stained.

'See if your poor mother could make that fit for inspection,' Sister said, sighing, and, lifting the specimen on the end of a ruler, looked at it from a safe distance and dropped it on the desk with what may have been a nod of encouragement.

Sometimes on a Saturday afternoon as we crowded the entrance to the picture house, waiting for it to open, a voice might cry, 'Holy God! The nuns. The nuns are comin'!' It was a signal for us to tumble into the shed next door until they had passed. Nothing they could or would have done to me, at least, could have been worse than stifling in the downy air and gagging on the smell in the shed. Women sat on benches in there, plucking dead hens flung to them by two executioners.

The men hung the birds upside down by tied feet on hooks secured to a lath nailed to the wall, nicked the necks with short, sharp knives so that their blood ran down to sawdust on the floor. The women held them between their knees and the limp necks and bloody heads jerked loosely as patches of white skin appeared under fingers snapping at feathers. The light was dim and the air was full of floating down from the feathers pushed into sacks between the pluckers. A few women sat on a form alongside a long narrow table. It seemed to me that they sat in the middle of a solid bad smell for the plucked hens were thrown to them to be drawn. They dropped waste into buckets on the floor and put gizzards, livers and hearts into basins on the table.

They seemed to understand why we wanted to keep our distance from the nuns, why we did not want to see them out of school and why we hid in the shed if we saw them coming. The nuns were always in twos. We liked to imagine their disapproval of 'The pictures.' It was part of the thrill, an introduction to the pending cliff-hanger to see a threat in the appearance of authority in our secret world of away; away from school, away from home, away from fathers and mothers, a way to escape. So we shoved and pushed into the cramped picture house for the pleasure of cheering the galloping cowboy as he snatched Mary Pickford up to his saddle from the railroad track where she had been left, tied up, by savage Indians just as the train came round the bend belching smoke.

Sunday dramas

You would imagine that we couldn't look at chicken for dinner knowing what went on in the shed but it was a different article altogether when Mother or Bridget had finished with it. Roast chickens were standard fare on Sundays. It was fun jerking the toes at each other by pulling on the ligaments of the cut-off legs as we young ones hung around the kitchen. We argued as to whose turn it was to pull out the tough pin feathers with the pliers. There were no arguments as to who should burn off hairy patches over a flaming paper on a tin tray. Grown ups, only!

A thorough wipe with a clean damp cloth left the fowl ready for stuffing with a savoury mix of chopped onion cooked in plenty of butter, chopped parsley, thyme, the chopped livers, bread crumbs, salt and pepper and an egg beaten with a little milk, all worked together. It was spooned into the birds' cavities and neck ends, the 'pope's nose' slid through slits in the overlapped upper skins of the rear end to secure it; and the crops well filled for it was essential to have plenty of stuffing to eke out the precious flesh for division between so many.

The thighs rested comfortably against the plump sides when the drumsticks were tied under the pope's nose. Fatty rashers moulded over the breasts and haunches, tied down to keep the wings in place, gave a dapper, almost smug, look to the birds sitting on the roasting tin, ready for the oven. That wonderful Sunday smell permeated the entire house every time the oven door was opened for basting.

'Very important,' Mother said. 'Keeps the flesh moist. Nothing worse than dry chicken.' She wasted few words when she was cooking. Carrots were scraped, not peeled, and cut into faggots, then cooked in as little water as possible with a sliced onion, a couple of cloves and salt. They were cooked when the point of her special knife told her they were. 'Keep that drop of water for the gravy,' she might order a helper as she shook the drained carrots in butter with a shake of pepper and sugar in the hot pan before putting them in a dish in the low oven.

No one ever cooked turnips as she did. Cutting them into cubes, boiling and mashing them was a prelude to the real preparation. A length of ticking, kept for the purpose, was scalded and spread on the table. This was folded over a portion of turnip and the ends twisted tightly over a bowl to catch the drops of water until all the turnip was 'dried' and tossed into a fresh pot with a knob of butter, pepper and salt and a grating or two of nutmeg, then vigorously beaten over the heat. It looked a work of art spread in a pie dish with a forked design on its golden surface.

What a lot of butter mother used! It was no wonder that her cooking tasted so good or that we grew up to be so finicky about food. She bought the week's supply from the same two women at their stalls in the Square on market day. She always tasted and if one woman's butter was on the salty side the other's would be a shade too mild. She never complained to them, for, as she said herself, she knew where it came from and she could always do her own blending.

The butter women packed up early for they could be sure that what didn't sell quickly wouldn't sell at all. They knew that all depended on how the pattern-inscribed pound slabs were set out on the well-scrubbed boards and on the neatness no less than the whiteness of the muslin that wrapped them around leaving only the print on view. A suspicious person might tell you to stick a needle through the print for fear a water-filled hollow might deceive you in the weight, or a buttery shell enclose a cake of mashed potato. But that sort of fraud must have happened a long time ago, if it happened at all, for Mother said she never heard tell of it in her time.

On the odd fine Sunday in summer there was great excitement in the market square when the brakes arrived to take the big boys and girls on a picnic to Esker Lough. A brake had room for sixteen, eight a side, and it took two horses to draw it. It was a sight to see when two or three of them drew up opposite McAleer's hotel and filled up with girls in big hats and flouncey dresses and boys in their luvisca jackets, some, such as the bank clerks, wearing swanky panama hats.

It took them a long time to settle themselves, what with making sure that the food and crates of lemonade were properly packed under the seats and the crockery safely wedged. It was the girls' job to organise the eatables and drinkables, enough for everyone, not forgetting the drivers. They wouldn't thank you for sandwiches. Baked ham, a roast of beef, a roasted fowl, a crock of salad, a plum cake, jellies and a trifle were the order of the day. Breadboards and carving knives and everything needed to eat with and to eat off were brought and, of course, teapots and kettles. The boys had to bring their own cups.

They brought no strong drink for if they did no girl would be let go again. Anyhow, what they never had they never missed. Half the Catholics in the town gathered in the Square after late Mass to watch them starting off and to admire the horses. They were done up for the day with ribbons plaited into their manes and tails. Their harness brasses glinted and jangled as they tossed their heads and snorted, wanting to be off. The Catholics pitied the poor Protestants, never let out on the Sabbath except for three times to church and Sunday school, passing by on the other side of the Square with their Bibles under their arms and trying to ignore their neighbours' unseemly behaviour.

When the driver got the nod to start there'd be great cheering and laughing because the jolting over the cobbles would throw the boys and girls forwards and sideways and forwards against each other and that's why the girls hung back from getting into the brake, pretending they'd forgotten a kettle or something, to make sure the boys took their places first. There was an art in getting to sit opposite whichever boy was favoured.

The boys got their turn when they all went for a paddle in the Lough. There were leeches in the water, not many, but now and again, when a girl paddled out, she would see two or three fastened to her leg. That gave a chance to a boy to come running to her rescue when he heard her screaming. Many's the fellow made a bad start that way, for it was a serious business for a boy to handle a girl in public and well the girls knew it. Some of them weren't above pretending to have leeches on their legs. The trick was to put a lighted match to the leeches' heads to make them lose their hold. Sometimes a girl would lead a fellow on and run when she saw him coming with matches at the ready. The race might end in a tumble in the bushes. It never amounted to much for all the fuss at Confession the next Saturday night.

There were other ways of spending Sunday in fine weather.

Boating on Carlingford Lough

The boys played in school football teams and might cycle off to play matches in nearby townlands. Or they might sneak up to St Patrick's Hall to smoke cigarettes and play billiards. It was quite a regular thing for three or four of us to be taken for a drive in the big open Armstrong Siddley motor when Mother put on a hat and sat beside Father at the wheel. There was no question of Mother's learning to drive. That was a male prerogative.

While we squirmed on the back seat the parents sat upright in front unaware that, as we made our stately progress out of the town, we pulled faces at people we didn't know or didn't like and waved wildly at everyone else. Out of the town and into the country we settled down to enjoy the bumps and bounces as the motor rattled along on the uneven roads. No matter what road we took we stopped at someone's house to pay a visit for Father was a very gregarious man.

The friend would very likely be a farmer for the point of going for a drive was to go to 'the country'. The hazards encountered on such visits were formidable. We were warned to be quiet, to say 'Please' and 'Thank you' if we were offered anything to eat, to eat whatever was given to us whether we liked it or not, never to ask for more of what we did like. Dogs were God-sends. The grown-ups were usually so engrossed in serious gossip that it was possible to feed the pet under the table with the runny boiled egg, 'fresh from the nest,' or a slice of salty bacon, home-cured, of course.

Milk, warm from the cow, was a particular horror. On one Sunday I remember, I had to swallow a glass presented as a special treat. With Mother looking directly at me I could hardly refuse it and felt compelled to add 'That was lovely' to my 'Thank you *very* much.' When I was forced to accept a second glass it was no help that Mena escaped the ordeal by saying plainly, 'No, thank you. Milk makes me sick' and got fizzy lemonade instead. We were told that we could go as far as the fence to see the new foal in the field beyond the orchard. It must have been Autumn for the trees were laden with apples and pears.

I regurgitated the milk into a clump of nettles and followed my sister who was taking bites from the ripest looking fruit hanging from the branches. She was tall and had access to rosier apples and yellower pears than I. Still the pleasure of leaving the mystery of the bitten fruit was a cause for hilarity all the way home. And I had savoured sweet revenge. Milk, warm from the cow . . . Ugh! Having to drink it compounded the terror of a challenge, on a visit to another of father's farmer friends, to try my hand at milking. The rhythmic swish of the creamy stream as it squirted into the bucket was soothing in a way. It was the physicality of the exercise which revolted me.

It was always I who had to endure these ordeals. I was anxious to please, subservient, and full of curiosity. My sister could look, assess, decide whether or not to accept an offer, pursue a suggestion, or usually, say 'I'd rather not, thank you,' leaving me to wish that I had been as honest. For all her ladylike ways she could climb like a lizard and run like a hare. She loved to spiel a lamppost and sit, like Simon Stylites on his tower, on the cross-bar at the top, a feat she was expressly forbidden to perform. Reported or discovered she would be ordered 'To bed, miss, and no tea,' by Mother who could never see such a sentence through and paid no attention when Mena sidled into place at the tea-table.

Our Aunt Rose lived outside the town in a pretty house with a large garden. She was Mother's sister. Her husband had 'an official position' in the Royal Irish Constabulary which was pensionable but badly paid. He was quiet and gentle. He respected and admired our aunt and adored his two children, our cousins, whom he called Tomboy and Girlie.

Their mother and father rather looked down on our thriftless businessman father who enjoyed life and loved to put on a show and left his large family to the unstinting care of our mother. Our uncle advised our brothers to 'make a prisoner of every penny'. But he was not a mean man. He was saying that money is the passport to success in this life. He dug his garden and grew vegetables and asked nothing for himself. Our aunt practised domestic economy to the nth degree. Their house smelt of new-made bread when we sometimes called on a Sunday and she gave us tea and slices of her own brown bread, never cake. She dressed classically in Irish tweeds in pastel colours and when she came into the market square on market day she carried a silver-handled ebony walking stick. We died of embarrassment when she came to the school at the nuns' invitation and talked about Anna Parnell, Charles Stewart Parnell's sister. She had preached self-sufficiency, that everyone should keep a goat to provide milk and to make cheese from the surplus, if any.

Our aunt's and uncle's one aim was to put their children into 'the professions', to give them security for life. Along with their hens, the goat was an important item in their economy. It cost almost nothing to keep for its tether allowed it a daily circumference of grass and saved Uncle James the bother of cutting it.

Mena never ran so fast in her life as the day she decided to take the goat for a walk. Its collar was tied by a rope to the ring of a tether driven deep into the ground with his sledge hammer by Uncle James. It wasn't easy to dislodge the stake. The goat watched, its yellow eyes gleaming, as Mena worked at it, pushing the ring backwards and forwards and rotating it. When it loosened she stood over it, wrapped the rope a couple of times around her wrist and pulled.

The stake shot up and Mena sat down. The goat saw its chance and took it. It bolted out of the gate, jerked her upright and dragged her belting after it. It was long enough before she had the wit to let go of the stake and when she did she sat down again. The goat stopped dead in its tracks and sauntered back as if it really had been out for a stroll. Mena was still sitting on the ground when I got to her. She was too astonished to cry and perhaps a little bit shocked but she got up and walked off in a huff with me for laughing myself silly.

She depended on me though, not to tell. Our conspiracy was shared by the cousins who led the goat back and managed to tether it in its place as if it had never left it. They lived a terribly quiet and protected life and loved the minor dramas we created if only by our number and our need to fight our corners and establish individual rights. They were in awe of our brother James, who set the whole county talking about him. One summer Sunday he 'borrowed' our brother Phauds' car to go to a picnic at Warrenpoint and was giving a lift home in the early evening to two sisters he had met when heavy rain began to fall.

The wet road glistened and he saw no difference between it and the surface of Carlingford Lough which lay ahead. There were no barriers to stop him. He drove straight into the water which covered the car by a foot or two. He used his head as a battering ram to make a hole in the roof, climbed through it and dragged the panicking girls after him. They slipped from him into the water but he managed to hook a finger into a cheek of each of them and yanked their heads above water. Fortunately, some people were returning from evening devotions and heard his shouts. He and the girls were soon bundled into a rowing boat and hurried to dry land and mugs of sweet tea by a hot fire in the police station. Much was made of James's heroism but his first concern was our brother's reaction to the car's ruin. This, in a day or two, took second place to his alarm when the girls' mother wrote to Father demanding that James should marry one of her daughters, he having 'got her name up.'

'Serve her right if he did,' Father commented sourly.

Ardboe

Sometimes we drove to the Old Cross at Ardboe to visit our Great-aunt Kate and Uncle Michael, mother's brother. We always referred to the Old Cross and never to Ardboe. Mother got irritated if people pronounced the 'd' and were sharply corrected and told

The Old Cross of Ardboe

to say 'Arboe'.

The Old Cross commanded the entrance to the cemetery, where graves had spread through the ages around the ruins of a monastery viewing Lough Neagh. Our mother's family vault is near to it. It is described by Polly Devlin in her book *All of us there* as 'the grandest of all graves and the most terrible and bleak. This is the Treanors' tomb, a marble platform reached by a shallow flight of steps with a copy of a Celtic cross surrounded by railings on top. It is falling to pieces but it still has a shocking decayed grandeur.' The memorial has since been restored by the family.

The vault is cased in panels of white marble with the names of the interred inscribed in black. Its high cross is impressive if not actually pretentious. Uncle Michael died of a fall from the roof of his house as he inspected a workman's repairs to it. His widow, Lizzie, a Devlin, was a beautiful woman, with blue-black hair drawn into a loose knot, who sat over a turf fire smoking cigarettes all day and colouring like a kipper.

After Michael died she became almost totally reclusive and re-fused to admit Mother and Father and whichever of us happened to be with them when they came to call. She left what little re-mained of the family fortune to a nephew from Glasgow who arrived out of the blue one day and cajoled Lizzie into admitting him. She died soon after and the old house, the last on the road nearest the graveyard, within sight of the Lough, was sold. It became semi-derelict and was suspected of being used as a hide-out by the IRA. The British Army wrecked it. The ground floor, covered from end to end by good quality tiles, became a byre for cows. Happily, it has since been restored with the carefully pre-served tiles re-laid.

I wonder if the kitchen tables of Ardboe have still the snowy whiteness and satin touch achieved by scrubbing with silver sand from the loughshore? And have the midges been eliminated by chemicals or are they kept out of the houses by inner doors half-panelled with sheets of minutely perforated zinc?

My maternal grandfather, James Emmet Treanor, was a mer-chant with many interests. He bought and sold flax for the linen business in Dungannon and in Belgium. He owned a bakery, a public house, and the Battery Hotel on the Lough's western shore. 'The Battery' superseded the official name of the place, Newport Trench. It was a busy port. Merchandise and fish transhipped from it and in the process procured steady custom for the hotel. Other attractions were lauded by Grandfather and although I don't remember him I take pride in his reported appreciation of Lough Neagh as a source of physical well-being and cultural potential.

According to him, a premature death was escaped by many 'by taking apartments at Newport Trench and spending the summer months along the beautiful and romantic shores of Lough Neagh.' It was, he said, 'the only spot in Ireland that sets at defiance the general debilities which follow the human system.' He cited no scientific authority for his assertion that the waters of the Lough

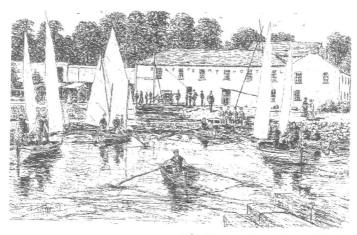

The Battery Hotel, Lough Neagh

had the power of transmuting wood into stone and his positive claim that the atmosphere contained a greater percentage of ozone than any other yet explored. He assured cyclists that the roads along the Lough's western shore were all they could desire and that the landscape provided artists with a real paradise to paint, instead of an imaginary one.

Grandfather's gift for hyperbole was inherited by his grandsons, one of whom perpetrated the myth, among many, that he sold horses to the Czar of Russia and delivered them in person in Petrograd. This is probably as true as the boast that Great-aunt Kate was the best horsewoman in Co. Tyrone. There was no evidence of this accomplishment in my memory of her, a dim figure who had nothing to say to us, lying under a Paisley shawl on a sofa.

Eels from the Lough were a staple of our diet and we always brought home a supply, in a box full of wet grass, its lid well tied down, to toss into a barrel of water in the yard. Bridget had no patience with our horror of them as she caught hold of her choice from the thrashing, flashing mass and chopped off its head with her cleaver. She expertly slipped off the slithery skin like a stocking and stuck it on a nail in the wall. Its sinister writhing long after its separation didn't impair our appetites in the least. Mother cut the body in pieces and stewed it in an infusion of milk and onion and fresh bay leaves thickened with butter and flour and seasoned. She was convinced that eel, a most gelatinous dish, made our hair thick and glossy and our nails and teeth strong.

In season, going to Ardboe, we pinched our noses against the stench, hovering relentlessly, which made us retch. It came from the fetid pools where flax was laid to rot from its tow and expose the fibre for scutching and beetling in the mills marking the stages in its preparation for spinning into linen. The bleaching greens, where lengths of the spun fabric were spread to whiten, were part of the landscape we took for granted as we drove along. One of the pleasures of these outings was the bumpiness of the roads which bounced us off our seats and rocked and rolled us from side to side.

Pink coats

Mother was fashion conscious and liked to see her daughters dressed in an approximation, at least, to the latest fashion. We were growing and when she decided that Mena and I needed new coats she evidently thought the task of making them, at that particular time, to be beyond her. She sent us down to Miss Brown, the dressmaker, who lived over Annie McIllhatton's sweet shop in Church Street. The shop was a small narrow space with a counter cutting it in two between the wall and the shelves behind holding jars of gobstoppers, jelly babies and the usual teeth rotters that we bought pennyworths of on our way to or from school.

Bunches of liquorice laces hung on nails in the shelves. My own penny favourite was a liquorice pipe, the business part topped with red hundreds-and-thousands simulating burning tobacco. It lasted a long time if the stem was only sucked and was good value for a penny but the temptation to bite was strong. The delicious taste of a chewed inch of it was addictive so that while my companions were swelling one cheek and then the other as they savoured a bull's eye or a brandy ball sliding across their tongues I was reduced to exploring my teeth with the tip of my tongue for any little pick of liquorice that stuck in a crevice.

We all loved 'yalla man', the porous toffee made by adding vinegar and bread soda to boiling sugar. Annie McIllhatton kept a tray of broken pieces at the far end of the counter near the door into the kitchen. The boys weren't above helping themselves to one when we crowded into the shop. It was enough reason for her surly manner. No one had the nerve or the heart to tell her that the toffee stuck to the newspaper pokes she put it into nor how it picked up the print and ruined a paragraph in the *Tyrone Courier* about, say, how Tosser Irvine attacked Kelly's dog with a graip, as well as dirtying the toffee.

Miss Brown sent a message to Mother for Mena and me to come to be measured for the coats and again for a fitting. We had to go through the shop into the kitchen and up the narrow wooden stairs from it to Miss Brown's room. We were afraid of Annie McIllhatton and wasted no time; in and up, down and out as fast as we could.

Miss Brown measured for length, measured for sleeves from shoulder to elbow and from bent elbow to wrist. She turned us this way and that, stuck pins here and there and sometimes pricked us. She tacked the linings together and pinned them into the coats. She put them on us and stood us on a chair to level the hems. We had to put our hands through slits in the side-seams to make sure of the right height for the pockets. The fronts crossed over and fastened at the sides with ties of the material, the fashion of the moment. The colour was dusty pink.

Came the day when the coats were finished. For some reason we had to have them in a hurry and were sent to collect them when it was dusky but not yet dark. The door opened easily when we turned the handle. It was eerie inside the shop in the unusual quiet. The jars of sweets and the bunches of liquorice laces threw weird shapes into the dying light. We crept to the kitchen door and slowly, slowly opened it. There on the table lay Annie McIllhatton cosily wrapped in an eiderdown, her white hair loose all over a pillow, either fast asleep or pretending to be.

That was shock enough, but worse was the sight of her big black cat curled on top of a mound of 'yalla man' under the table, contentedly purring. Terrified of waking either we tip-toed up on feathered feet and collected our parcelled coats. Safely reaching the street again we took to our heels and laughed all the way home competing to be the first to tell mother about the cat on the 'yalla man.' Needless to say, we lost our taste for it.

Such dresses!

My mother rarely left the house and she loved to hear the harmless gossip we brought home to her. But the Devil never found work for her for her hands were never idle. The pity is that her creativity never got the recognition from her children that it deserved. We took it for granted but loved to watch her when she made posies of roses from butter, making petals and leaves with deft slaps of the wooden pats, rolling small scoops of it into thin stems or flattening some of them into ribbons to tie the posies together. She turned out wonderful things for the grown-up brothers' and sisters' annual party such as boats made from bananas with triangles of wafers for sails, put to sea on stormy waves of meringue.

She knitted and crocheted petticoats, cardigans, jerseys, the petticoats mitred, the cardigans strengthened with tightly knit bands for edging and double knit elbows, the jerseys jollied with marching ducks or alert rabbits knitted in, in appropriate colours. She crocheted Roses of Sharon into deep lace borders for fine linen altar cloths for the occasional priest acquaintance to take to some far-off mission. The old Singer sewing machine, mounted on its ornamental cast iron stand, seemed to generate a never-ending hum as she turned sheets from sides to middle, patched table cloths and sewed what she loved best to make, our dresses.

Such dresses! With what pride Mena and I wore the lettuce-green flounced ones of finest nuns' veiling trimmed with delicate lace Peter Pan collars. There was one she made for me of brilliant white cotton piqué. I wore it on a hot summer's day going for gooseberries with a basket to Beatty's down the Donaghmore road. Picking them was hot work and the basket grew heavy as I walked home. Nothing more natural than to sit on that nice little patch of grass at the base of the telegraph pole to rest and to enjoy a ripe gooseberry or two. Back in the town I preened when I saw people pointing at me as I walked up the street, confident that my dress and I made a lovely couple.

I swung jauntily into the kitchen and heaved the heavy basket on to the table. Joe came out from under it to see what had caused the thump overhead.

'Your back's all black.'

His voice was flat as he sniffed a faint whiff of tar. I twisted and saw the edge of a black stain of tar extending from my shoulder to below my waist. My dress was ruined. Those people pointing had been making fun of me. I was mortified. Mother looked at me with that twitching smile of hers.

'The pole. It must've been the telegraph pole. The tar must've melted. I only sat down for a minute or two.'

'Long enough,' was all she said. She lifted the dress off over my head and I started to cry when she bundled it up and stuffed it into the ragbag for the tinker woman. She gently told me to go upstairs and put on my white and red check, a dress she knew I hated; but I suppose it was her way of teaching me to be more careful; more effective than giving me a scolding or complaining about the waste of material and her time and trouble in making the white one.

I felt mutinous and vengeful. Mary Ann Madden. Danny Wherry. Laughing at me! Joe looked on, enjoying himself. His red hair was tousled as usual, a grin on his freckled face, his hands grubby.

'Come on, you,' I commanded and he followed obediently as I left the kitchen.

Two sisters kept a tiny haberdashery shop between Green's the butcher and Hughes' dairy in Scotch Street. Mother often sent Mena and me to them for spools of mercerised cotton and hanks of knitting wool. We never wanted to take Joe with us because he never wanted to walk back from anywhere but would stand still, stubborn, and demand to be 'callied' all the way home, but sometimes we were ordered to, and to take him for a walk.

The sisters loved to see him. They sat him up on the counter and flirted with him, young as he was, three or four or five, while he regarded them gravely from round grey eyes. We pretended to disgust when he puckered his lips to give them a kiss for a penny before we left. So I settled on Joe to extract satisfaction from the world in general for my humiliation. Mena joined us on the way down the street. I explained my strategy and she agreed to play.

'We're just taking wee Joe for walk, Miss McCann,' I said to one or other of them for they were both Miss McCann to us.

'And we brought him in to see you,' Mena chimed in.

To say that they were pleased is to put it mildly. They picked Joe up, sat him on the counter. They admired his jersey with its three ducks and the hole in the elbow. They ruffled his hair and pulled up his socks. They tied the loose lace of one of his gutties. We wished they'd get on with it. Mena nudged them.

'We have to go now, Miss McCann.'

'Ah, well, so. Give us a kiss Joe, and we'll give you a penny.'

'Give me thixpence and I'll give you two,' he lisped as instructed. He closed his eyes tightly and puckered and nearly spoiled the game by purposefully thrusting out his open hand.

'Well, well, well. Aren't you the great wee businessman altogether.'

Although Miss McCann looked doubtful she dipped into the cash drawer, withdrew a silver coin, and wrapped his hand around it. He jumped off the counter and stared at it.

'It's not thix pennies,' he wailed. 'It's . . . It's . . . '

But Mena had jerked him out the door before he could say more while I warmly promised the Misses McCann that we'd never bring Joe in again. He was getting out of hand so he was. Bridget had him spoiled so she had, I babbled as I backed out.

We gave Joe a big penny for his miserable wee sixpence, but fair play, we did give him his share of broken biscuits that Mrs Connolly let us pick ourselves from the glass-fronted tins on the stand in her shop. It was a matter of honour not to break biscuits on purpose nor to take only the fancy ones and leave the Mariettas because Josephine Connolly was in my class and I liked her.

Belfast

Our father drank too much, not all the time but in bouts. If he came home, 'under the influence', calling 'Nan, Nan,' Mother simply led him upstairs and put him to bed. She made a pick-me-up to cure his hangovers. Eggs in their shells in a bowl were covered with lemon juice. When the shells dissolved she beat sugar into the messy yolks and whites and when they were thick and pale she beat in some cream and brandy. She gave him a measure of the concoction several times a day for a day or two, with never a cross word between them, until he recovered his self-respect.

His business was in general drapery and wholesale linens. He dressed nattily and wore a gold chain, with an amber seal and gold toothpick attached, across his stomach. It secured his thin gold watch to his waistcoat pocket. He was a justice of the peace. A parchment, heavily sealed in red wax, authenticated this distinction. We became thoroughly ashamed of it as political aware-

Father and the hat.

ness dawned, especially as it became apparent that his power to jail the town drunks in Dungannon was ill matched by his own lapses. Then we moved to Belfast. I don't remember anyone telling us youngsters that we were moving; nor were we told why. Before the move Father had been a medium-sized fish in a very small pond. Now the big city pond was dense with shovers and pushers with whom he had either to swim or sink.

The effort, I think, distanced him even further from his children. I have no memory of his relationship with the older ones. I know that I never had a conversation with him. He must have noticed me because he called me 'Bunty,' as he called Mena 'Legs', but from a distance. I observed him, took him in, as it were, without any emotional attachment. But it was not the custom in those days for Irish parents to show affection.

'A decent reticence' was Mother's guiding precept by which she regulated our behaviour. A decent reticence enabled one to accept with dignity the role of a wife, mother and sacrificial house-slave as Mother did but with humour, too, and unwavering loyalty. Father once bought her a hat and we looked on gravely as he helped her to adjust the tilt of the brim before we set out on a Sunday drive. It was plain that he admired her as he stood back to study the effect. Queen Mary of England invariably wore a toque over her corrugated upswept hair. He thought the toque had run its course and that a change of style would benefit the royal image. He wrote to the queen to say so and was pleased to receive a reply from a lady-in-waiting to say that her Majesty had noted his remarks; but she continued to wear the toque.

The twenties and early thirties were a doleful time in Belfast. Linen and shipbuilding had been the staples of Belfast's industry, but they were rapidly succumbing to cheaper foreign competition. Unemployment was a common lot and poverty was rampant. Tuberculosis was widespread. Half the city was to let. Posters advertising premises plastered the walls and men stood in groups at street corners sharing cigarettes, sometimes showing off the fine points of a greyhound or swapping boastful stories about racing pigeons. Large signs in black wooden frames warned that the end was nigh, that *Vengeance is mine saith the Lord*. REPENT was a frequent command. Menace was dissipated by the cheery rattle of Salvation Army mandolins demanding attention to a preacher promising reward for virtue. 'Yes' the bonneted Army ladies sang:

> Yes, we'll gather by the river,
> The beautiful, the beautiful, river,
> Yes, we'll gather by the river
> That flows by the thro-one of God.

The King on his throne and God on his were reassuring figures

Molly, Kevin, Father and Nina in the garden in Sunnybanks, Antrim Road, Belfast

of power who would some day reward obedience with a vision of the mighty. Politics passed us by insofar as conscious participation was concerned; but we knew that the revolvers hanging from policemen's shiny belts were not for our protection, that Protestants despised us, and that Unionists wouldn't give us the light of day if they could help it.

In the meantime we had to go to school. Mena went to the Dominicans on the Falls Road where the annual fee was higher than my minimal one at St Patrick's Academy for Young Ladies in the Cromac area. I was again in the charge of the Sisters of Mercy and had the great good luck to have Miss Kerris for English class. She liked my compositions and sometimes read them aloud to the class such as the one on 'How I Spent My Summer Holidays'.

I described how I had to cook for my brothers because Mother wasn't well. They ate so much of the things they liked that I got tired of peeling potatoes for champ and Bramley apples for tarts, so I cooked the things I knew they hated like sago pudding with only a little dab of jam on each helping. Miss Kerris lent me books by Charles Dickens and now and again she took me for walks in the Botanic Gardens to talk about them. And she got me to sing along with her: 'All through the night there's a little brown bird singing . . .' She was a wonderful teacher, generous far beyond the call of duty, and I cried for a week when she left to get married.

I bought my school books in Ambrose Serridge's book and stationery shop, off the Falls Road, because a girl in my class worked there on Saturdays. Ambrose's significance for me had nothing to do with his shop. With four or five other young girls I used to go to the top of Cavehill on regular walks in his company. He was a gentle, determined man. He wore an old Donegal tweed overcoat with sagging pockets.

Those pockets are what I best remember of his appearance as we trailed around him up the hill. He herded us like an old hen. We walked and sat and stood as he talked and we listened. Sometimes we'd sit in a hollow when a heavy mist came down. It would drift in whorls and ribbons over our heads and, though we'd huddle together, each of us seemed ghostly, adrift in separate worlds. And Ambrose went on talking. He talked of things well short of a young girl's interest.

What was Henry Joy McCracken to me? Or Wolfe Tone, or Robert Emmet, or Henry Grattan, or Jemmy Hope, or Lord Edward Fitzgerald? What did I care about secret oaths, or funeral orations, or speeches from the dock? What *was* a dock? It was lovely up on the Cavehill. The clouds raced in the sky when it was windy, the trees made queer shapes and the ground was mossy, slippery when it was extra steep. So we put up with Ambrose.

Phauds

Him and his history! We never laughed at him, though. There was something about him that made us keep our distance. When he shared out the bruised pears, squashed plums and broken biscuits we ate them even if we didn't want to. His big pockets held an awful lot of paper bags and the ones that weren't wet with juice or torn, he'd blow up and burst with a bang. He'd hold the burst bag between his two hands and listen, listen to something that we couldn't hear. Now that he's dead and gone I wish I'd listened with more attention to what he told us.

In the beautiful Glens of Antrim

Sometimes Phauds took Mena and me, or Joe and Mena, or me and Joe with him when he went on his rounds through the beautiful Glens of Antrim selling Aga cookers to rich farmers' wives. We waited for him in the car listening to peals of laughter ringing from open windows as he told them funny stories and flattered them witless. He was just as happy getting the herring women in Glenarm to sing along with him when he'd stop and stay for a good half-hour and buy choice specimens of the fish to bring home to Mother.

The women loved to see him coming and called to him as he

got out of the car. Banter flew between them as bloodied hands gutted the slit herrings and threw them into barrels. It was a horrible sight and the work was unforgiving but the women rose to our brother's cajolery and sang with passionate good humour some such song as 'The Star of The County Down'. We sulked in the car, waiting for him to come and drive us away from the overpowering smell of fish and the sight of the herring women's red hands.

Phauds had a genuine interest in the life, the places and the people he met on his travels. He never failed to call on Samuel who lived in a tiny one-roomed cottage fitted snugly into the side of a hill near Glenarm. Samuel was a small ball of a man. He wore his house as if it had been made to measure for him for he could sit at the table in the middle of the room and simply reach for anything he wanted, or so it seemed; but then, he didn't want for much. He had studied and had a qualification in herbal medicine but his eccentric appearance and life-style put people off. Phauds was one of the few who took him seriously and was always greeted warmly by him. He loved to explain to us the uses of the withered leaves and wild flowers hanging in bunches from the ceiling and from nails in the walls. There were glass jars full of powders and some of wrinkled berries. Strings of apple rings and sliced pears lay on a metal rack fitted over the enclosed wood-burning stove, drying out for winter use. Pots of infusions covered the top of the stove. It exhaled the sweet scent of apple-wood ash with its mellow heat.

A burn of clear water burbled down the hill into and out of a small round pond Samuel had constructed from stones gathered from 'up and down the hill'. It was only big enough for a bath he told us, you couldn't swim in it, and he laughed when we shivered at the very thought of the touch of the ice-cold water. Samuel's skin was pink and his face shone with fresh air and cleanliness. Who knows what accounted for the gloss on his luxuriant long silver curls? We liked him. He never gave us anything to eat and contented himself with giving a bottle of mushroom ketchup for Mother in return for a half bottle of poteen to make a 'drop' of sloe gin for himself for Christmas. Mother praised the ketchup. 'Concentrated,' she said. 'You can't beat the wild mushrooms.'

A little culture

Music was mandatory in the curricula of young people trying to meet their parents' or rather, their mothers', aspirations for them. Mother was no different from the others who wished for a veneer of culture, however thin, to cover their children's natural want of gentility. She engaged Miss Summers to come to the house in Coalisland to teach the violin and the piano. Miss Summers was afflicted with a tooth which grew from the roof of her mouth. It affected her speech and it may have been this as well as Father's aversion to childish violin scraping and the boring repetition of scales on the piano which interfered with my brothers' and sisters' concentration. They made no progress but did grow to love music. Phauds, Jack and Nina sang well and had a repertoire of the popular songs of the time. Jack and Nina were inclined to be soulful and diligently practised their sentimental contributions to the Christmas entertainment of the workhouse inmates.

Rollicking tunes were more to Phauds' taste but he, too, could draw a tear when he sang folk songs of love and loss. Mena and Joe and Kevin and I loved to sit on the stairs to listen when their friends gathered for a party. We loved to join in, knowing we couldn't be heard, when Mickey Devine sang:

> Tell me, tell me, where are you roaming
> Shipmates of mine?
> The war is on and the great ships are sailing
> Shipmates of mine.
> Tell me, tell me, oh tell me your stor-ee.
> All fate has giv'n you
> Sor-or-or-ow or gloreeee?

And then we laughed ourselves silly trying to imitate him when he tried to match his voice to the words:

Down, deep down . . .

Mother's last hopes of a musician in the family rested on me, so when she arranged piano lessons for me in Belfast twice a week after school. I enjoyed the lessons except when the teacher called me 'darling'. The poor woman was just trying to encourage me. She said I had promise and I knew that I had a feeling for the nuances of the sounds but feeling was not nearly enough for command of the keyboard. Hard practice was impossible in the circumstances and I contented myself and disappointed Mother and the teacher with mastery of four party pieces including a passage from a Beethoven symphony, my favourite, but which I rattled off with the now forgotten others as if they were one. I got immense comfort from playing by ear, in the dark, lugubrious hymns and long-drawn-out romantic ballads.

I loved to hear myself sing, while I picked out the notes:

I am a young maid
And my story is sad
For once I was courted
By a brave sailor lad
He courted me strongly
By night and by day
And now my dear sailor
Is gone far away . . .

and so on to a tragic conclusion. I could make myself cry, or ally myself with saints and martyrs, happily sitting there at the piano in the dark. Such self-indulgence was a distraction from 'the tech', the Municipal Technical College, where I went to evening classes in shorthand and typing because, the nuns persuaded me, they would stand to me whichever path I decided to follow. The course included compulsory English and again I was lucky in my teacher.

Mother with Kevin (in front) and Joe

He was a Mr Figgis who, it was obvious, had a passion for books. He was never without one in his hand and there was always a stack of them on his table. He introduced me to contemporary English poets and lent me novels by, among others, the Brontë sisters and Jane Austen, and questioned me after class to make sure that I read them. He gave me literary magazines to read, he said, at my leisure. I took his interest for granted and would have preferred if he had taken less notice of me for I was too young to appreciate what he was doing, his efforts on my behalf.

The nuns were gently nudging me to the path they wished me to follow. They tried to persuade me to do 'The Matric', the examination for entrance to university. I was not to worry about anything. They would look after 'the arrangements'. I knew that they meant that they would pay the fees, buy the books. They would have known that the general economic depression hit our family as it did most others; but their kindness only alarmed me. To accept, I thought unworthily, would mean that I would have to join the order, become a nun. Secretly I had heard a call to a different vocation.

'Ssh. She's writing.'

The Abbey Theatre Company came to town. I read about it in the *Belfast Telegraph* and the *Irish News*. I would be an actress. I had no hope at all of getting to see the plays but I could, and I would, meet the players. It seemed the most natural thing in the world that I should take my oldest sister Molly's navy blue serge suit, try it on and decide that it was suitable for the part I intended to play. I carried a jotter and pencil for authenticity and presented myself at the stage-door of the Opera House, Belfast's only professional theatre, as a reporter from the *Irish News*, sent to interview the leading lady. The man who opened the door to me was tall, thin, bespectacled. He wore a white coat and, except for the claw hammer in his hand, he looked like a doctor.

'I'm Arthur Shields,' he said, 'I'm the stage-manager tonight. Can I help you?'

I was transported. I was, I had to be, a reporter.

'I'd like to interview Eileen Crowe,' I explained. He looked surprised and said something like, 'Well, yes, but she's busy just now. If you'd like to watch from the wings till this act finishes we'll see what we can do.'

Wings? Act? What was he talking about? He put his finger to his lips and led me, tip-toeing, to a dimly lit corner beside the stage where a woman was sitting on a stool. He whispered to her: 'May, this is a reporter. I'll come back for her' and left me standing beside May Craig, one of the famous Abbey actresses who was 'Prompt' for this performance. She, intent on the stage and the prompt copy of the play she held, paid no attention to me. I was enthralled, not even aware of a possible penalty should Arthur Shields find me out, should Molly look for her suit and find it on me. As the curtains slid to close, applause started, May Craig stood up, and the stage-manager appeared.

He beckoned me to follow him into a dressing-room, 'Vacant for now,' he explained. A Japanese kimono hung from a hook on the back of the door. Light grey trousers lay over the back of a chair. He picked a handful of clothes off the seat and dropped them on the floor and invited me to sit. He offered me a cigarette. I had never smoked. I took one, uncertainly, from the packet. He struck a match and held the flame towards me. I held the cigarette towards it but a sudden vision of general custom directed me to place its end in my mouth. I held it there between thumb and forefinger and inhaled deeply as the flame ignited the weed. Short shallow coughs expelled puffs of blue smoke towards him until I dropped the cigarette into the ash-tray he held beneath it and felt for a handkerchief.

A shelf on the wall held half-used thick coloured pencils, a large tin of what looked like lard, hair brushes, and a comb. A dirty towel hung from a mirror surrounded by light bulbs. The pencils were, of course, grease-paints and the towel looked dirty because it was used to wipe off make-up long before paper tissues became an extravagance. It must have been apparent to the actor that I was avidly curious as my gaze ranged the small room and fastened on the grease-paints.

'You can turn yourself into anyone with these,' he said and picked two from the shelf. He lifted my hand, turned it palm upwards and painted the face of an old woman with just a few strokes and rubs. He drew a doll's face on my other palm with different paints. I looked at them and at him. He looked at me. Neither of us said anything. He must have known that I was yet another stage-struck hopeful whom he would never meet again but to whom, being a good and gentle man, he must be kind. I went home in a trance, restored Molly's suit to her wardrobe and, to assuage my conscience, sat up half the night writing a eulogy of Arthur Shields. I sent it to the *Irish News* and to my astonishment, it was published and paid for with a cheque for seven shillings and sixpence.

Mother was thrilled and for a while afterwards she quieted any interruption if I was writing, even if I was only addressing an envelope. 'Ssh,' she'd say, 'She's writing.' Acting was another matter. What possessed me to think of such a thing, she wondered? and ordered Molly to come with me when the manager of a travelling company who had advertised for an ingénue, wrote to arrange an interview in reply to my 'esteemed application'. He asked me to read the part in a play which involved an eviction scene. I thoroughly enjoyed putting on the pathos.

It was a pity that there was no one to play to besides Molly and the man. Neither of them applauded when I finished reading although they did go very still while I performed. The room was nothing like the little of the stage I had seen in the Abbey. A billiard table filled the middle of it. There were benches against the walls. A stale, heavy smell of cigarette smoke hung about and the few naked light bulbs strung over the table had no relation to the imagined glamour of footlights.

I felt depressed and must have looked it for the man put his arm across my shoulder.

'You'll do,' he said.

Molly took over.

'We'll let you know when she's available,' she said firmly and, holding my elbow, she marched me out and home.

I didn't need to be told that that was the end of that. Molly's report to Mother resulted in one of her wily judgements, designed to achieve her end yet avoid confrontation.

'You don't have to bother him again,' she told me. 'The cheek of him to think we'd allow you to go round the country with him and his troupe without even asking our permission and you under age. What would the nuns say? Plenty, if you don't do your exercise! Just look at the time!'. Exercise was what is now known as home-work. I was pleased enough to get out my books, secretly grateful that, for now, I was safe in the family fold.

2 Vocations

ONE BY ONE the older members of the family drifted away—to America, to England and to Dublin. Mena had set off to see the world via a cottage hospital in Coleraine. There she discovered in herself a true vocation for nursing. She was advised to apply for full training at the General Infirmary at Leeds. It was the largest teaching hospital in the North of England and is now known as the St James University Hospital. The first three months were spent with fifteen other recruits studying the theory and practice of nursing in the Preliminary Training School. After an examination and an interview with a psychiatrist, those of the probationers who had passed were given their separate rooms in the nurses' home.

Her scrappy letters home ('practically asleep . . . too tired to write more . . . have to go now . . . ') described a regime with every hour and minute of the day accounted for in a time-table regulated by the strictest discipline. Sometimes she mentioned a picnic on the moors or having been to the pictures. It had been a lovely day, but windy. The picture had been good or no good. Her friend Gerry had got a parcel from home and had invited a few of the set to a little party in her room. 'The set,' we gathered, were the trainees.

No ceremony accompanied their introduction to actual patients whose diseases had formerly been presented in rubber models, by diagram and photograph. Real male and female skeletons introduced them to practical anatomy and physiology. Those poor bones were strung up like victims of rough justice. They were a source of great hilarity to practical jokers who sometimes dressed them exotically in a mix of garments or pressed cheap luminous watches into the eye-sockets, designed to scare the life out of anyone who happened to wander into the dimly lit lecture room.

I slowly realised that the parents trusted Mena, were proud of her and I began to think I could make her my key to freedom. But: 'A nurse? You?' Mother simply refused to discuss the idea. It never occurred to me that she might miss my help in the house which was seldom free of visitors. There was no end to the cooking and changing of bed linen and though life in general was agreeable enough I was working hard and getting no nearer to my secret goal. I would have to get away. Leeds was the obvious springboard. A strategy, sub-consciously devised, was successful. I just talked as if a nursing career was my dearest wish; that entry to it via Leeds and Mena's sponsorship was assured. I wrote to the Matron. She requested me to send a birth certificate—I was nineteen—and a reference from my headmistress. Mother Mary Madeleine, who had resigned herself to the improbability of my joining the order, wrote that I was diligent and capable which, apparently, with Mena as model, was all it was necessary to know of me.

When a letter inviting me to present for admission to the Preliminary Training School arrived, Mother suddenly accepted the inevitable and began to assemble uniform and accessories according to an official list which accompanied the letter. I had no sense that she might grieve for loss of the company of the youngest of her daughters or how quiet the house would be without 'Annie Laurie' or 'Danny Boy' sung loud and clear as I made beds or cooked a meal.

With a frilly-capped Ward Sister, another probationer, and a student nurse

I tried hard to squeeze a few reluctant tears from my eyes when I left but they wouldn't come. I just couldn't wait to get away. I had an insatiable curiosity about life apart from the one I knew and I was fortified by the ignorance of youth. For the first time in my life I felt a person, an independent grown adult. Travel on a real big boat across a real sea and a train journey towards the drama of life in a hospital was surely half-way to my goal. My brain whizzed like a cine camera and every single incident of that momentous journey made its imprint so that seventy years later I can still conjure the smell of a B & I cabin and feel the damp but thrilling chill of a dawn-time arrival in Holyhead.

I don't suppose a more naive aspirant to the nursing profession ever crossed the threshold of that enormous hospital. There were eleven Catholics among the three hundred nurses of all other religions and none. In 1932 there were no black nurses. I remember just one black doctor. He had a beautiful white smile and the child patients loved him. Most of the Catholic nurses were Irish but were dispersed in order of rank and duty rotas so that we seldom met. When we did meet we found that we had little in common. One, from Tipperary, asked me if I was the new 'Arish' girl. When I said 'Yes' she asked 'Do you hant?'

We shared allegiance to our religion and a strong nationalism which surged to the surface when prejudices about our Irishness were expressed by our English colleagues. It was assumed that we had fiery tempers and were ridden by superstition. Most surprising was the discovery of bigotry which I, at least, had thought to be confined to our Orange brethren at home. A chapel on the premises served the needs of the Protestant staff but we Catholics had difficulty in getting to Mass in time in the town when an adjustment of ten minutes between night and day staff hand-over on Sundays would have been a simple and satisfactory solution to our problem. Ever the rebel, I made my own arrangements with friendly junior staff and got to Mass feeling not only the promise of holy martyrdom but noble patriotism as well.

Fortunately, our set included enough oddities to dilute the strength of any local bigotries some of us may have harboured. May Wong Lee from Hong Kong arrived with a moon face suffused with good humour and a trunkful of beautiful clothes. When our arguments got out of hand she chided us with mild reproaches in an impeccable Home Counties accent; 'Oh gels, please, *please* don't bickah.' She had trained to be a professional pianist, she told us, flexing her long ivory fingers, but had tired of the solitary hours of practice. The parents of a girl from Hull were in shipping and enormously rich, according to gossip. Hilda kept herself to herself and it was scarcely noticed when she quietly left to marry a Sir Something in York.

Letty had graduated from an art college in London. She wanted to specialise in medical and surgical illustration and where better to find models for practice than in a general hospital? She was a Cockney, a shrewd little businesswoman. It wasn't long before she attracted the attention of consultants who commissioned and paid for drawings of exposed symptoms of their patients' diseases. She learned, as we all did, the practice of dove-tailing and might be found behind screens drawing a woman's leg ulcers having given her a bed-pan. She carried her sketch-book in the bib of her apron.

The St James University Hospital at Leeds

The patients were fascinated by her transference of their blemishes to paper, her turning them into things of beauty in coloured pictures. They shared her intense concentration and emotional detachment while she worked and unwittingly fostered some pride in their contribution to medical research. There was no use in speaking to her. She ignored interruptions and carried on, although she did take time, once, to emphasise to me the value of observation of detail.

Members of our group were individually interesting but we were too busy to cultivate each other or to form best-friends attachments; we went through our four years' training, it seemed, at breakneck speed. In her letters home, Mena had forborne to mention the existence of a parallel set of medical students who entered the wards at the same time as we did. Ward sisters, staff nurses, our mentors, impeded with unceasing vigilance any attempt at liaison but nature took its course and engineered enough chance encounters to enable us to plan illicit meetings. We had one day off per month, one half-day per week and two hours daily, but we had to attend the same lectures in medicine and surgery as the students besides lectures in nursing practice by sister tutor. And we had to study in our off-time.

Came a day when I declared that I had had enough. I would leave. I have a vague memory of honey-coloured flagstones paving a cloister-like passage alongside wards. As I strode along, feeling mutinous, I was surprised by a group of students who surrounded me.

'Leaving, are you?'

'You can't, you know.'

'It's not the sort of thing one does.'

'Giving in isn't really in your line. Is it?'

'You'd be ashamed. Afterwards.'

'Terribly insulting to patients. You'll tell them?

'Of course if you're ill or there's family trouble . . . '

This was solicitous. I astonished myself by shouting: 'Oh, go to blazes.' I stayed.

One of the students, Marcus, was tall, blond and handsome. He had a slight limp from having had poliomyelitis in childhood. It was no handicap for it joined his good looks in rousing maternal as well as romantic yearning in the hearts of most women whose path he crossed. Not in mine. The lure of the stage obsessed me still and I fantasised in the daily drama of hospital life. Marcus shared a cottage on the Yorkshire moors with three or four other students. The cottage was small, square, built of stone. Its most memorable feature was a wide-mouthed jar on a window-sill on a landing. When the wind from the moors blew over it through the open casement it made a deep mournful sound.

They were such innocent and happy times. Marcus and I lay on the heather and recited to each other all the poetry we could remember and half-remember. Once he kissed the back of my neck. I pretended not to notice. He was English; not a Catholic.

Back in the cottage when it was time to tidy the kitchen I washed a carving knife and was told never, ever to do such a thing again. A carving knife must never be washed, only wiped. An Irish faux-pas or English vagary? I thought of the carving knives I boiled in the steriliser every day.

Marcus was a member of an army officers' training corps. He invited me to his division's annual dinner. What to wear? It had to be long, long-sleeved, long skirted. I owned no such garment. May Wong Lee produced one from her trunk, a dark blue velvet affair, square-necked, beautifully cut and fitting me well enough except that it was a shade too long. Still, grasping the side of the skirt and lifting it slightly added to the effect I had on Marcus as I descended the wide stone stairs to where he waited to greet me, with approving eyes, before the huge fire-place in the front hall.

He looked unreal in uniform and, for once, I was wordless. He looked taller than usual due, perhaps, to the tight dark trousers and the scarlet braid running down the outside seams. The jacket was a splendid affair. We were on our way to a pre-war Tolstoyan party in Moscow, I decided, and must have puzzled Marcus by my sudden change of accent; but, in no time, he abandoned me to a crowd of women in a ladies' cloakroom all of whom seemed to know each other and who called loudly for safety pins to make minor adjustments to petticoats and waistbands. They suddenly took off like a flight of birds and swept me with them into a large room, its walls decorated with regimental flags and portraits of crusty old men wearing medals.

Long tables looked wonderful dressed in white damask, flowers, lots of silver, lighted candles, glinting wine-glasses and cut-glass decanters. That was all very well but where was Marcus? A man with a list in his hand asked my name and indicated a chair just as I spotted my cavalier at a distant table standing between two seated women.

We waved despairingly at each other and I sat down. With a great scraping of chairs the men seated themselves. The elderly man on my right immediately started to quiz me. He had been to Ireland many times. Mostly West. Loved the place. Charming people. Fishing. No? Nursing. A *most* useful occupation. Take you anywhere, y'know. Talk of war. Need 'em all.

He spoke in short sharp bursts, like a machine gun, and I suspected he was a high-up something in the army. He had a place in Scotland. Deer. His wife preferred the house in London. Theatre and all that. He talked about plays, actors he had met. He put away the machine gun and talked more normally as *I* quizzed *him*. Dinner was served. We stood with everyone else when silence was prayed for and a toast to the King was drunk. The men lit up their cigars and the women their Passing Clouds. Time was passing. Speeches began and went on and on. I grew more and more uneasy for I had to clock into the hospital by eleven.

I whispered my dilemma to my companion.

'Just slip out,' he said kindly. 'I'll see to Marcus.'

The hem of my skirt had caught under a chair leg when I sat down. As I moved away the chair came with me making an unholy racket in the bored hush. Everyone looked towards me. Lord Whatshisname had leapt to his feet to release my skirt. He took me by the arm and propelled me towards the door. This must have been taken as a signal, for everyone else, more than eagerly, rose and followed us. I wrung the good lord's hand and raced to the cloakroom for my coat. Marcus caught up with me on the street. He looked apoplectic. With rage? He leaned on the bonnet of the little Austin in a paroxysm of laughter which he controlled only when I thumped him on the back and yelled the time. This was a minor drama.

Major ones, sometimes tragic, occurred on the wards. An explosion in a coal mine could kill or disable men for life. Explosion injuries were difficult to deal with. Flesh, deeply and raggedly torn, had to be cleaned of coal dust and fragments of coal extracted. A worse than usual wound in a thigh had hydrogen peroxide poured into it to float the dust up in the bubbles while a nurse and a doctor trapped it in sterile swabs. My job was to cut off the man's vest while they worked. It was grey and felted with sweat but despite the blackness of his face, neck and hands, the skin of his body was pearly white. Only his clenched fists betrayed his agony before he was given a sedative by injection and taken to the theatre for more invasive repair.

We shared sincere sympathy for such a man and his relatives and felt real grief if he should die. Yorkshire folk were down-to-earth, stoical, independent and kind. They worked terribly hard and I think they appreciated that we, too, worked hard. Anyhow, we responded well to each other and it pleased us immensely when an explosion victim walked from the ward with his family. Sometimes I had the sensation that I was acting a small part in a play when the plot was so intensely sad and urgent that the suspension of belief was an imperative.

It was unusual for the Sister in Out Patients to come to the ward with a case but on one occasion she came hurrying in alongside the trolley. Tom, the porter, looked grim. Ward Sister swung the screen aside from the bed, all ready with its water-filled mattress and its emergency trolley beside it. The Sisters exchanged glances, their faces expressionless. I was ordered to help. As the four of us carefully lifted the sheet with the woman onto the bed some of her skin came off on my arms, black wrinkled shreds that stuck. She was badly burned.

It was evident that she couldn't live. Her face was white, her eyes wide open. She seemed to stare at something in the far, far distance, something that had nothing to do with her present plight. Whatever it was she stared at couldn't have been unpleasant for her look was soft, almost tender. She said nothing. She made no moan. Her hair was black on her brow, wet with the perspiration which framed her face in tiny beads. They covered her with a bamboo cradle and drew a sheet over it so that nothing should touch her. Then the doctors came and I was told to wait outside.

The case was one for staff more experienced than a mere probationer. I felt useless.

A man stood at the ward door and I guessed that he had followed the woman. He was a miserable specimen, about thirty-five years of age, raggedly dressed, thin, dumb from shock and trembling. I took his hand and led him to the armchair at Sister's desk and sat him down. I reckoned it was not a time to keep a rule however strict. I took a key from a drawer in the desk, unlocked the medicine cupboard, poured a measure of brandy and gave it to him. I didn't know what to say to him so I started a round of temperature taking.

A few beds down, I heard Sister call me. 'Take this to the sluice room,' she ordered. Alone in the sluice room I lifted the cloth. The tiny unmistakable baby was curled up in the kidney dish. I did what I felt I had to do, then covered the little body and left it for Tom to see to. Back in the ward, Sister was leading the man to the small side-ward used for patients' relatives to rest and be comforted after a death. She signed to me to attend to him while she spoke to the two doctors. They were relaxed now that it was over and the mother, fortunately, gone, for even had she lived, she'd have had no life.

'What hope?' one of them said. 'Living in a tent! Lucky the whole family wasn't caught in the blaze.'

The man had shrunk in that short time. I held his trembling hands but could think of nothing to say to him. What could I say that would make any difference?

'It was a boy,' I told him, at last. 'I baptised him. Was that all right?'

He slipped to the floor and with his head between his knees he wept for a long time. Sister said to leave him, to get the bed ready for him and go to the dining room to get a hot supper for him.

'We'll get him to bed when he's had his supper,' she said, 'and I'll give him something to make him sleep. The whole tribe'll be in on top of us the minute they know where he is. They'll take over, Lord help them.' Then, remembering that I was only a probationer to be kept in her place, she told me sharply that my cap was crooked and my apron an absolute disgrace.

Our training included all the hospital disciplines, ear, nose and throat, eyes, children's diseases, medical and surgical cases and casualties. Optional courses included fevers and tropical diseases, and obstetrics and midwifery at the Women's Hospital. We took case histories, temperatures, blood pressures, blood; gave injections, dressed wounds, removed stitches from eyes and post-operative cuts of all descriptions. We administered medicines and filled in charts. We washed patients, gave them bed-pans and bed-baths, and dressed and fed them when necessary. We comforted them and bolstered their confidence.

We answered their and their relatives' questions with discretion telling them no more than they needed to know. And we kept our distance. Emotional involvement would have made it impossible to do our job. Cheerful detachment was the order of the day and if we were sometimes called 'hard-hearted Hannahs' we put up with it. Our earliest injunction in the Preliminary Training School was that the hospital was for the patients, not the staff, and that we probationers counted for less than the dust.

It is difficult to convey the stringency with which protocol was applied to rank. By now Mena was a senior staff nurse with the special cachet of working in the theatres. Our paths rarely crossed. I had to attend lectures and to study during my off-duty hours. Her social life included occasional dinners in top restaurants with senior medicos while mine was confined to outings on the moors with small groups of student nurses and medical students as poor as I. (We nurses were paid five pounds a month, quarterly!) Still, it was a comfort to know that she was never far away and we did manage to have a meal together sometimes. And I remember that once she thought I looked tired and put a DO NOT DISTURB notice on my door on my day off. I slept through the entire day and night and awoke buoyant and refreshed and grateful.

I was content to limit my term to the four years (1932–6) necessary to earn my silver and mauve enamelled badge, state registration and a claim to graduation from the Royal College of Nursing of London. I was invited to stay on to train in radiology with the prospect of a senior position in the X-ray department, than which nothing tempted me less. I had suffered waves of desperate home-sickness and now I was free to go home. I had my own agenda.

A wonderful world

Basil had gone to Dublin where he worked with Cahills, the printers, and shared a flat with a barrister friend in Raglan Road, a swanky part of the city. Soon after my return to Belfast from Leeds he invited me to visit for a weekend but I went on a day excursion. I wasted time tracking him down and then getting over the shock of his new way of life. The door was opened by a maid in a black and white uniform. She showed me into a sitting room and sat me down beside a table with magazines on it.

'The master will be with you in a minute,' she murmured respectfully.

Who did she mean? 'The master?' Basil? Master? The brother? I could hear Mother, shaking with laughter, saying: 'Basil! You

Basil and I, conniving

couldn't be up to him!'

We lunched at a round table in a bay window looking out on a tree covered with pink blossoms. A small flat arrangement of primroses sat in the centre of a white linen table-cloth. The flat-mate and his girl arrived. He was chatty and fidgety and she was languid. The talk was of politics and rugby but I was so taken up with the menu that I paid little attention to it. We started with stuffed tomatoes on toast and I knew by the display of cutlery that there was more to come, so I had to bite my tongue to prevent myself from remarking that with a bit more toast, they'd be the main course at home. Roast chicken followed. I must have been wide-eyed at the fat sausages around it not to mention Basil's expert handiwork with the carving knife. Chicken *and* sausages! And a maid! No question, Basil had come up in the world, and he had Dublin to thank.

The three left me to the station in the barrister's Baby Ford. The languid girl gave me two bars of chocolate to see me home. The barrister bought me a *Belfast Telegraph* and Basil gave me a story, *A Young Man From The South* by Lennox Robinson, to read on the train. A tiny flame in my psyche still burned with a suppressed passion for theatre, the Abbey Theatre in particular. And the Abbey was in Dublin . . .

I started, with Basil's connivance, to cajole the parents into moving to Dublin. Pa, as we called him, had retired from business and was only too ready to taste the leisurely pleasures of the south. Mother was tired out though gallant as ever. She suffered from constant pain, which doctors were unable to alleviate, from cancerous ulcers on her legs. She claimed relief from folk cures her sons, especially Jack, persuaded her to try. Dock leaves, bread and buttermilk poultices and God knows what creams and lotions dreamed up by wise women in the depth of the country were brought to her with loving hope. Nothing worked and she was glad to move to the distraction of change, away from the unease of life in Belfast with its underlying menace.

We moved in 1937 to Drumcondra. By now there were only five of us at home: Jack, Phauds, Nina, myself and Joe. Daniel, whom I hardly knew for he left home when I was still a child, had gone to America; Molly stayed in Belfast where she managed a restaurant; Martin, Mena, James and Kevin were all in England and, of course, Basil was in his flat in Ballsbridge. Our large house on Clonliffe Road was early Victorian with characteristic steps up to the front door. I loved it for the two trees which grew in the front garden on either side of the stone steps and for the thrush—or was it a blackbird?—which sang so gloriously from the branches of one of them outside my bedroom window. The city hummed at my elbow and the Abbey was a tuppenny bus-ride away. Radio Eireann, on the top floor of the historic General Post Office, was within walking distance.

Now in my twenties, I was the quintessential girl-at-home, the daughter who does the housework with inadequate hired help, looks after the old folk, welcomes for holidays the emigrant siblings, visiting relatives and friends; and somehow finds time to pursue her own interests which, however important to her, will always bow to family needs. Mother never demanded anything of anyone. Her one lament, sometimes expressed in exasperation, was that we had no ambition. This was her northern work ethic fulminating against Father's western (he was from Leitrim) laissez faire. It was reprehensible in the north not to be ambitious. To be ambitious in the south was to be pushy, cute, devious.

I sensed that acting fell far short of sensible ambition in family opinion. 'Who do you think you are?' a brother asked me, 'Norma Shearer?' It didn't matter to me who or what I was. All I knew was an ardent desire to be someone other than myself, a transmogrification only acting catered for. I thought that the Abbey School of Acting would open up a new and wonderful world to me if only it would admit me as a student. As it happens, I was right. It did. I went for audition and was accepted.

But there were fees to be paid. As it was unlikely that anyone else would be willing to pay for what must have seemed to them to be sheer self-indulgence I decided that, somehow, I would pay them myself. Molly, second eldest of the family, oldest sister, and therefore to be absolved of interest in my lowly affairs, nevertheless encouragingly paid for the first term. The publication of 'the' interview with Arthur Shields was an impetus to earn some money by writing. Subjects lay under my nose. I wrote a piece about my first encounter with Lennox Robinson and it was published in the *Irish Press*. I used a pen-name, Mother's maiden name, Anne Treanor.

The audition has been given, I have received notice to attend and, at last, after all these years of hankering I am a student of the Abbey Theatre School of Acting!

That first morning was a curiously cold-blooded affair. Somehow, I felt just ordinary when I expected to feel nervous, quite flat when I should have been thrilled and slightly brazen when modesty should have conquered me. Mr Lennox Robinson, a long, thin man in blue, is friendly but turns out to be surprisingly efficient and disciplinary.

We were standing there outside the Peacock Theatre and he asked us if we minded waiting a minute, quietly. There was a rehearsal in progress and presently Shelah Richards, very neat in a black two-piece and hatless; Cyril Cusack with that shy whimsical look about him; Fred Johnson, charming in untidy tweeds, and Hugh Hunt trooped down the steps and away and then it was our turn.

Mr Robinson beckoned us in. He told us to sit down just anywhere. He called the roll but I heard no name but my own and I saying 'Yes' in a strangled voice. There are about twelve girls in my group and one lone man whose friend is yet to come. I wondered why there were so many females. Were we more artistic? Or more stage-struck? or (disappointing thought) was it just that we have more time on our hands? And I thought, how many of us will stay the course? and does everyone here want to act or are they teachers inter-

ested in voice production and deportment?

*. . . We are to do quite a lot of verse-speaking for the good of our
voices–to produce beauty and depth and power. We had to stand on
the stage, individually, and read poetry and be corrected about enun-
ciation, rhythm, nuance, and so on. I had Tennyson and to me my
voice sounded raucous and far too loud and the thing just didn't
make sense.*

*After a while we sat in a semicircle and read a play, cast at ran-
dom to give Mr Robinson some idea of our powers of characterisa-
tion. Most of us thought we had not much use for faery fantasy—
good lusty stuff like* The New Gossoon *or* The Playboy of the Western
World *was more in our line but, sure, that wasn't for us to say . . .*

'I Go On The Stage' *Irish Press*, 30 September 1937

Lennox directed the school and was its principal teacher. He was
a favourite butt of impersonators of the time, an easy target with
his long, thin, angled arms, long, thin gesturing hands and his
long, long legs tied in knots or disentangling themselves from an
impossible embrace with chair legs. His surprised eyes compelled
attention from behind thick lenses. A back view gave him the
head of a boy. He was a true educator in the sense of drawing out.
He told us about work in the hayfield at the end of a long day so
that we felt prickly and hot, drowsy and tired. An imaginary bucket
filled with imaginary water dragged one sideways with the weight
of it. The balancing movement came automatically as a hand
brushed the hair off a forehead.

As he talked the picture became complete and the actor's personality transmuted into that of a village gossip, a worrying mother
or faery child according to the demand of the play of the moment. He never said 'Do—or say—it this way,' but patiently chis-
elled into one's being like a sculptor using suggestion as a tool
until the creation emerged. It soon appeared that the adjuncts to
acting in the art of the theatre—voice production, movement,

make-up, history of the drama, costume—subjects taught by experts in the Royal Academy of Dramatic Art in London and the Comédie Française in Paris, were not taught in the School. Ours not to reason why. The geniuses who had matured in the Abbey still controlled it.

However, students had the right, provided it was discreetly exercised, to explore the theatre and to familiarise themselves with every aspect of stagecraft. Not all of us were sufficiently interested to bother but I was intrigued by the hidden mysteries which contributed so much to the magic of the productions. Tanya Moiseiwitsch was the exotic name of the person who worked wonders in 'the paint room' and I resolved to have a look at what went on there and at the presiding priestess.

I went up the stairs off-stage, past the Green Room, past the wardrobe rooms, through a short corridor of dressing rooms, straight ahead and there it was. An immediate impression was of a young woman with a blue-spotted scarf around her head showing a rim of black hair, Madonna style, large dark eyes with a small, perfect mole under the right one and tall slimness clad in navy dungarees lightly spattered with green and white plaster off a tree she was 'dressing' for a stage set. And that was Tanya Moiseiwitsch.

Paint was everywhere, in buckets on the floor, in cans on the window-sill, in tins on shelves and in enamel mugs on a long table in the middle of the room and the little round one at its end, not to mention a splash here and a blob there. Mixed up with paint-pots and other paraphernalia of the designer's craft—brushes, pencils, paper, a half-finished model were an aluminium kettle, a blue jug, a yellow tea-pot, a pound pot of raspberry jam, and a cup and odd saucer on an orange tray. Over all hung the pungent smell of glue, redolent of the Abbey's ambience.

I also explored the Green Room, the most sacrosanct room in the building. Yeats spent time there. So did Lady Gregory when she left Coole in Galway and came to Dublin on Abbey business.

It wouldn't do to intrude on them when they met there for tea with, perhaps, other members of the board. Neither did actors like to be disturbed when they spent time in it learning lines or having to be sociable in the intensity of listening for a call on-stage. However, I learned that the best time to visit the Green Room was about an hour-and-a-half before a performance when actors would more than likely be in their dressing-rooms and the panjandrums would have left. My visit resulted in an article published by the *Irish Press*, and another term's fee.

Years of longing were consummated in the cold kiss of black American cloth as I pushed back on the sofa and began my acquaintance with the Abbey from a player's angle, as I wanted to know it. The green of its walls was faded but restful as it was meant to be. It was a cosy, intimate room, comfortable and friendly. You wouldn't mind dropping ash on the coconut matting on the floor or a newspaper out of your hand and not bothering to pick it up or putting a wet glass on a small round black table because there were so many marks on it already another couldn't possibly matter.

You might catch Lady Gregory gazing at you from behind the china clock on the narrow mantel shelf over the gas fire. You may feel inclined to smile at her but don't be deceived: Those large eyes of hers, which have lured several men of her choice to her bed, are capable of freezing the presumptuous. This is her territory. Trespassers are persecuted. You can't help but smile at young Willie Yeats's supercilious expression in the small portrait to the left but you become properly respectful in reading fragments of his genius, framed and hung on the slatted wooden wall.

At your elbow in the corner is a brass standard lamp, its pink silk shade slit here and there by senile decay. Roving to the left and upwards you take in pink roses—artificial, very familiar, perhaps from frequent stage appearances as a wedding bouquet, a centre-piece, on the brim of a hat. For now, they are in a glass vase on top of a black oak dresser. There is a tin of Marie biscuits on the jutting cupboard and cups and saucers with a glass jug full of milk. On the wall to the right of the dresser James Stephens looks introspective as if in the throes of composing The Crock of Gold *or listening to the sudden cry of pain he wrote of in a poem about a trapped rabbit.*

Arthur Shields, also behind glass, is telling the story of how he murdered his Da in the character of Christy Mahon in The Playboy of the Western World *while the great F. J. McCormack looks villainous as Rabbit Hamill. Fred O'Donovan dominates a delightful bronze of the Sergeant and the Patriot in Lady Gregory's* The Rising of the Moon. *The script room (no more than a cupboard) and a book case flanking the door at right angles tell the history of the Abbey in play titles. All the successes are there with the might-have-beens, the good attempts and a great deal of George Bernard Shaw.*

There are caricatures and photographs of unfamiliar faces and old group photographs of the company taken on tour in America. There are conventional studio photographs of Lennox Robinson, W. B. Yeats and Padraic Colum; but the real character studies in this Green Room are the chairs and the chintz-covered sofa opposite me. Used looking and sagging, they have received the ischial tuberosities of many of the most famous men of letters of the past and present generations. All the players, at some time or other have dug themselves in to study lines or talk to friends or just to sit.

Life's alternatives

Lennox Robinson sometimes invited a group of us to his house, Sorrento Cottage, overlooking beautiful Killiney Bay. As we arrived he would hand each of us a small round rush mat to sit on, on the floor. He explained the lack of a view from the sitting-room windows of the renowned Irish Bay of Naples as due to sea-spume which forever blew against the glass. Introductions to Sylvester, his dog: Johnston, Mooney and O'Brien, the canaries, named after the well known bakers; and numerous slinky cats were more demanding of our attention than our surroundings but I do retain an impression of chintzy comfort.

Dolly, Lennox's wife, an artist, gave us tea with brown bread, sandwiches and cake. She was plump, kind, unobtrusive and imperturbable. Someone remarked on the flavour of the tea. 'Unusual and very pleasant,' I said. Lennox told me to ask for Lapsang and Indian in Dermod O'Brien's special mixture in Freddie Fox's shop on St Stephen's Green. O'Brien was President of the Royal Hibernian Academy and of the United Arts Club. But Mr Gerard Smyth, Fox's tea-blender, told me that Mr Robinson always bought the Lapsang Suchong and must have made up the mixture himself.

I was learning that life is full of alternatives. The choice was open and one could, if one wanted to, put an individual imprint on every little detail of life. During and after tea Lennox guided the conversation around books and plays we may, or may not, have read and seen or even heard of. He was in no way intimidating. He dwelt, for example, on *The Doll's House* and how it exposed the hypocrisies of society and its entrapment of women. We became argumentative. He teased us to give reasons for our opinions and so forced us to think. In this way he introduced us to such writers as Ibsen and may even have been arousing our interest in foreign plays he would later produce for the Dublin Theatre Guild in which we might play a part.

Our class included Wilfred Brambell who became famous as the father in the popular BBC comedy series, *Steptoe and Son*. Maureen Fitzsimons joined us for a while before she became Maureen O'Hara, film star and millionaire business woman. Pale, gentle Val Iremonger gave no hint of his later career as poet, diplomat and Irish Ambassador to Sweden, Portugal and India. Frank Biggar became Ambassador to Switzerland. Norah Lever left to act and to produce independently. Phyllis Ryan won accolades in leading parts in the Abbey and for her productions when she formed her own company.

Eithne Dunne, Brian O'Higgins and Liam Redmond became

notable in Irish theatre and some succeeded in films in Hollywood. Daniel O'Herlihy was taken to Hollywood's heart. Stardom sat easily on that handsome head. I asked him what was in the briefcase he always carried.

'I'll show you,' he said. 'Always be prepared,' and he opened the case to display numerous studio photographs of that head taken from every angle, even from the back. I thought of him ever afterwards as 'The Head'.

Anne Yeats, daughter of the great W. B., joined us for a term or two. She was shy to the point of desperation, but her sense of humour was Dublin's at its best when she forgot herself. Perhaps the School helped her to find her true métier in painting. I have fleeting memories of her father, a heavy remote man with a pugnacious thrust to his lower lip. I might glimpse him backstage on a first night or walking down the aisle from a back seat in the theatre after a rehearsal. I don't recall that he ever spontaneously spoke a word to one of us and I can't imagine that any of us would have dreamt of speaking to him. Mr Yeats was master of the Abbey.

Lennox Robinson arranged for me to meet him, saying, 'He likes to meet promising students.' I am small and he was tall so it was hard for him to see me. In that haunted voice of his he spoke over my head: 'I understand that you are from the North.' He flapped a hand and turned away. Was I again being told that I was less than the dust or did he hear the rattle of old bones in Tullynish, Co. Down so rarely, if ever, acknowledged by him, where his grandfather had ministered so long ago? What Mr Yeats's theatre could do for me or I for it was in abeyance. His brother Jack the painter was different, an easy, jaunty man. He sat beside me once, in the Peacock, the Abbey's adjoining experimental theatre, during a rehearsal, and was silent or not as the mood took him in a comfortable, companionable way.

We students often helped the stage-manager by prompting or sorting bits and pieces used to furnish the stage set. It felt good to be useful and it felt especially good to be associated, however dis-

Cyril Cusack

tantly, with F. J. McCormack, Eileen Crowe, Maureen Delaney, Harry Brogan, Denis O'Dea and others of the greats whose miraculous creations interpreted Ireland's literary genius and brought it to world attention.

Cyril Cusack was becoming established in this distinguished company when I made his acquaintance. He was playing the lead in Louis D'Alton's play, *The Man in the Cloak*. 'The Man' was the poet James Clarence Mangan. One night, after the show, Cyril invited me to go for a walk and years afterwards, when I was writing a weekly column for *The Irish Press* I wrote a short piece about it. I wrote it in the third person.

The night was beautifully mild and balmy. . . . Dublin was not nearly so prosperous as it is now and at that time of the evening there was little traffic. Remember, it took time for the actor to change and to remove his make-up, so it was late enough.

Cusack had a habit of becoming so immersed in the role he was playing that he actually seemed to change personality and to assume the very character of the part. That night he was Mangan. It seemed natural that he should lead his companion towards the quays.

He shambled slowly along, his shoulders bent. Sometimes he made crab-like sorties to the waterside and peered short-sightedly into the river but mostly he hugged the walls and windows of the shops and houses. Sometimes he stood in a doorway and braced himself against it and groaned softly before tipping himself out again and moving on.

All the time he talked but he breathed so shallowly that it was often hard to catch his words. In any case, the little breezes from the river blew them about. Certainly he was telling stories of Mangan's old Dublin and, too, he would now and again break to a deep musical note and speak in the poet's words right to the end of a poem.

Was it by accident or design that the words

> *And Spanish ale shall give you hope*
> *My dark Rosaleen*
> *My own Rosaleen*
> *Shall glad your heart*
> *Shall give you hope*
> *Shall give you health and help and hope*
> *My dark Rosaleen*

urged them into Winetavern Street? By some trick of light the air was blue. Christchurch was blurred by it and it gently joined itself by scarves of vapour to the crescent of old shuttered shops on Michael's Hill.

The actor and the girl stood to rest a little, and to look, under a street lamp. The place seemed heavy with dream when suddenly Cyril became himself.

'I stayed there once or twice,' he said, pointing to a window over a shop. 'It was years ago, when my step-father, Breffni O'Rourke, and my mother were touring. I could never get to sleep with that damn lamp shining into the room. Come on. I'll race you down the hill.'

She caught up with him over the bridge at the Four Courts. Three swans, motionless on the river, caught their attention. And then, like

an explosion over their heads, the dawn racket of birds awake fright-
ened them into time.

'My mother!' the girl cried. They ran to O'Connell Street. He
bundled her into a cab, and in new roles, bowing and waving royally
to imagined crowds, they clippety cloppetyed home. (8 May 1964)

I went for another walk with Cyril on a summer afternoon after a
matinée when he was playing the Blind Man in John Millington
Synge's *The Well of the Saints.* As we set out I had the temerity to
praise Michael Dolan in the role in an earlier performance. I really did think that Cyril's need to project a sympathetic aura on to
his creations was inappropriate to the Blind Man whereas Dolan's
natural irascibility asserted his indifference to approbation. Cyril's
performances, in general, angled for a little sympathy for his characters, however unworthy of it they may have been. He liked to
be liked, on and off the stage, a human weakness which must be
universal.

My mild praise of Dolan was not meant as dispraise of Cyril
but it annoyed him. And to what an extent! We walked up the
quays towards the Phoenix Park. He paced himself to be slightly
ahead of me so that I felt like a tinker woman following her man,
as he probably meant me to feel. He parsed and analysed the text
of *The Well of the Saints* to the last comma. He'd stop in his tracks
to emphasise a point insisting that I agree with it. Whether I did
or did not made no difference; he'd resume his leading position
and proceed to prove the point of his reading of Synge's intention
as against Dolan's.

In this manner we reached the village of Lucan and, to my
infinite relief, he led me to a public house where he said we could
get some tea. He ordered rashers and eggs, sausages and bread
and butter with it and we ate in silence. My feet were killing me
for I was wearing new high-heeled shoes for which I had paid
thirty-seven shillings and sixpence the day before. I was too angry
with myself for not having had the wit to cut the walk short after

a hundred yards or so; and too proud to confide that the heels of my shoes had worn down to sharp angles and that the side of one of them had split.

When it was time to go I somehow rose and propelled myself out the door and along the road. There was no question of taking a taxi. Telephones were few and far between so I couldn't ring home for help. I knew that Shank's Mare was Cyril's only means of transport and he must have emptied his pockets paying for the tea for he was not yet an Abbey star. (Abbey salaries were minimal anyhow. Even those of his colleagues who were famous had day jobs to support them, a fact never mentioned in later years when part-time actors were derided as amateurs. No one could say of Cyril that he was an amateur. He had been born and brought up among professional players.)

The odd thing was that acting was the last thing he wanted to do, or so he told me as I tottered painfully behind him. He wanted to write; but my only concern just then was to hobble, if I could, as far as the tram terminus at the Phoenix Park. It was bliss to sit in and agony to get off the tram in O'Connell Street and board a bus, alone, for home. It was heaven to throw myself on my bed, let the ruined shoes fall off my feet and sink far down into the deep well of sleep.

Cyril's circumstances greatly improved as his status rose and his genius as an actor was recognised. He was helped by his easy assumption of his rightful place in another Ireland, a world away from the lives of most theatre-goers but to which the Abbey sometimes pointed a direction. I was surprised one day, when, for some reason, I attended a rehearsal of a play in Irish to see him cast in the leading role. *Casadh an tSúgáin* by Douglas Hyde was the first play in Irish to appear on a professional stage when it was produced in 1901 by the Irish Literary Theatre. Hyde had been elected President of Ireland in 1937. Now, on 19 August, 1938, his play was to get a second performance in his honour before a world audience at the Abbey Theatre Festival.

Hugh Hunt, who was English, produced it. He worked from a translation helped by Ernest Blythe who was a passionate promoter of the native language. I noted that Blythe corrected Cyril: 'Emphasise the *lá*—remember you're a Munster man now.' Most of the players, including Cyril, continued to speak 'the language' as they left the stage. He told me that he had first heard Irish spoken in Dungarvan when he was about five. He picked it up as he toured the country, a scrap here and a scrap there. Sometimes he learned it in schools, and, as a boarder in Newbridge, he had a longer period of more concentrated tuition; but he was always sufficiently interested to study a little and to read on his own. He spoke Irish whenever he had the opportunity as when he met native speakers in England or in America. I wrote an article about the rehearsal and *The Irish Press* published it on 4 May, 1938 earning me yet another contribution to the term fee.

Meanwhile I thought I was on my way to stardom when, towards the end of 1937, I got a note from Hugh Hunt written on official Abbey paper bidding me to attend a rehearsal of *She Had To Do Something* a new play by Sean O' Faolain which opened on St Stephen's Day. It was disappointing to find that I was one of a number of students similarly summoned, but at least I had a speaking part, as one of the dancers. The play is about a French woman who brings a troupe of Russian dancers to a town in Co. Cork and the effect an exotic culture has on its inhabitants. The lead part was played by Evelyn Bowen, an English actress, whose husband, Robert Speight, was playing in *Murder in the Cathedral* in New York while Bowen was in London,

Frank O'Connor, the writer, was managing director of the theatre, appointed by W. B. Yeats in 1937. O'Faolain and O'Connor, both born in Cork, were close friends. Evelyn Bowen was O'Connor's mistress so it was not too difficult to reason why she was cast to play the female lead in O'Faolain's play. The cast, especially the female members and most especially Shelah Richards, were furious at the casting of Bowen. They regarded it as a slur on their ability to play characters who weren't Irish. A strike was threatened. Only the consideration that theatre staff would lose wages, 'and it Christmas', prevented it. Hugh Hunt, in his history of the Abbey, explained that O'Connor argued that a strike would be interpreted as an act of discourtesy to a guest. A scholarly diversion.

We students had no idea of the undertow of bitterness affecting the production. We sympathised with Evelyn Bowen, a stranger in a strange land, at Christmas time. We decided to present her with a token of our good wishes on opening night. As fresh flowers would be unavailable we settled on a box of embroidered Irish linen handkerchiefs. I was deputed to present them after the dress rehearsal. I was also deputed to ask Hugh Hunt, on behalf of all of us, what we were to wear for the performance.

I think we had notions of high leather boots and furs suited to Siberian weather. At the rehearsal Hunt wore brown corduroys, a brown and beige tweed jacket, and a yellow shirt. I wore a brown tweed skirt, a checked tweed jacket and a yellow silk blouse with floppy bow. When we came to the end of the rehearsal and as he still hadn't volunteered costume instructions to us I piped up and thus drew attention to myself from the rest of the cast. There was a silence. At last he said: 'Oh, any tatty old thing. What you're wearing will do.'

That was a blow but, even so, I crossed the stage to where Evelyn Bowen was standing and handed her the box saying that the students wished her luck and a very happy Christmas. On opening night the curtain rose on the troupe dossing down on the floor of a room in a lodging house shared by all of us. I spoke my line, loud and clear:

'Oh, shut up!'

It was directed at my fellow dancers and also at the audience to let the play begin.

Not surprisingly, *She Had To Do Something* was a flop. It was

'Any tatty old thing . . .'

heartily booed. It never had a chance. And, not surprisingly, it was a long, long time before Shelah Richards could bring herself to speak to me.

Her niece, Pamela Fitzgerald, was a memorable student in my class. She lived with her family in a house overlooking Herbert Park. Her mother, Brownie, a sister of Shelah's, was indefatigably hospitable. Her house and garden were always full of family and friends. Her dining-room table was no sooner cleared after one meal than it was set for the next. She was recovering from an illness, when, one day, Pamela invited me for lunch. I had thought to bring some flowers for Brownie but had given the bus conductor a pound for my fare, all the money I had on me. He would give me change when he collected fares on the top deck but I forgot about it. I got off the bus at the top of Dawson Street and only remembered when I saw the bus sailing round the corner.

I ran but realised that I had no hope of catching up with it. A man came out of the University Club on Stephen's Green and opened the door of his car. As he got behind the steering wheel I sat in beside him on the passenger seat and, without a qualm, ordered him to: 'Follow that bus.' While I anxiously tried to keep the bus in sight it began to dawn on me that I should explain to this stranger what I was up to. 'Tell you what I'll do,' he said, 'I'll leave you at the bus-stop ahead of it.' He did and I left him with many thanks and apologies.

I got my change but had no flowers for Brownie. She declared that my story was better than any flowers and weren't Dublin men wonderful? 'Indeed, and indeed, they are,' I heartily agreed. Sad to say, I lost touch with Pamela later when one or the other of the many 'war efforts' claimed her generous heart. Someone told me that she had married an English officer, a Buddhist, who had lost an ear in combat. The leading character in the novel, *The Christmas Tree*, by Jennifer Johnston, her cousin, is based on Pamela.

By my third term in the Abbey School I was being offered parts in various productions. I played a leading role in May 1938 in a popular comedy, *Thompson in Tír na nÓg*, by Gerald McNamara, with the Father Mathew Players in the Father Mathew Hall in Church Street. Jack Cruise, who later made his name in variety theatre, played a part. A large photograph of me in a newspaper illustrated a favourable review of our performances. These productions were amateur, produced for the benefit of Capuchin/Franciscan charities, so Lennox made no objection to my extra-curricular forays.

Another time I played Deirdre to Robert Mooney's Naisi in a radio production of John Millington Synge's *Deirdre of the Sorrows*. Lennox invited the poet-playwright, T. S. Eliot, to 'the Station' as Radio Eireann was then called, to listen to it. When it finished I found myself being introduced to one pale-faced, bespectacled, tall, thin, elegant figure by another, Lennox. I was small and shy and ignorant and I hurried away from under them arching over me, all unaware of intended criticism or compliment.

The arts industry

The Abbey Theatre Festival in August 1938 gave a glimpse into the theatrical and literary industry inhabited by critics, talent spotters, financial backers, seekers of notice by association. Fourteen plays by the Abbey's most distinguished playwrights were performed in the theatre and there was a reception at the Municipal Gallery of Modern Art, excursions to Glendalough, to Tara and the Boyne Valley, and a series of lectures in the Gresham Hotel. The speakers were A. E. Malone, Frank O'Connor, Lennox Robinson, F. R. Higgins, Brinsley Macnamara, T. C. Murray, Walter Starkie, Denis Johnston, Ernest Blythe, and Michael MacLiammoir.

Lennox invited some students to help as official Festival hostesses. It would be hard to convey the earnestness, the dedication to Art for Art's sake, the innocence the visitors brought with them from far away places. We were supposed to introduce them, as they wished, to local celebrities. I wasn't prepared to be treated so respectfully because I had, metaphorically speaking, touched the hems of the Abbey's founders' garments!

Two elderly American ladies wearing toga-like tunics, barefooted in Grecian sandals, kept me captive in a café one night talking at me about comparative art forms through endless cups of coffee. I had no idea what an art form *was*! I felt a fraud but I needn't have worried. They said 'Good-night' contented to know that W. B. Yeats was a happily married man; that Maud Gonne was his muse, not his mistress; that she was not the Countess Markievicz but a completely different person; that the poet F. R. Higgins was, as they suspected, inclined to be bawdy.

They left me with a copy of a collection of Yeats's poems. They handed the book from one to the other as if it were the Holy Grail and then to me, requesting me with great intensity to have the poet sign it for them. He had not seemed to hear them when they asked him themselves—'so many people around him'. I took the book knowing full well that I wouldn't have the nerve to speak to the great man never mind ask a favour of him. I passed the buck to Anne, his daughter. Generously, she took the book but gave no assurance that she would be more successful than anyone else and in due course returned it with the paternal message that his autograph was his only capital which he had to conserve for posterity.

I was among a few students whom Lennox selected to form a verse-speaking class. The aim was to have a nucleus of verse-speakers prepared and practised to take part in future productions of verse-plays and poetry recitals and, I suspected, to fill walk-on parts in Abbey plays when needed. Lennox would occasionally invite visiting poets to hear us. Gordon Bottomley, an English poet, then in his sixties, was one of these. We were told that his verse-plays were successful on the professional stage in London, that he had been influenced, as Yeats had been in Ireland, by Celtic legends and early history and by Japanese Noh plays. Our recital for him and an invited audience was given in the Peacock Theatre. The programme had had no rehearsal and was characterised more by conversation among the auditors than by performance. I was, therefore, shocked when Lennox ordered me on to the stage and to speak a poem of my choice.

The only 'poems' I knew by heart were in the nature of recitations, party pieces not at all designed to impress a distinguished literary gent. It was even more disconcerting to see Lennox hop up the steps and out through the street door. Long afterwards I learned that his sudden dis-and re-appearances were due to what Lady Gregory had called his 'morbidity,' in other words his need for a quick drink. Anyhow, there I was, standing on the stage, staring into the distance, frantically trying to recall the words of a work worthy of the waiting poet.

> 'Is there anybody there
> Cried the traveller
> Knocking on the moonlit door'

I heard myself cry with muted anguish continuing to the end of Walter de la Mare's powerful atmospheric poem. Perhaps it was terror that removed me from that stage for I *was* that traveller. I smelt the horse's sweat and the smell of crushed fern on the forest floor. It was I who knocked on that moonlit door and it was I who yearned for the sound of voices and heard only the faintest of echoes.

If there was applause I didn't hear it and I stood for a moment or two while the trance passed. Mr Bottomley stood up. He said ecstatic things about my 'delivery.' I barely heard him. Lennox hopped in again, back to his seat. Mr Bottomley said what he had to say all over again at greater length. I cringed gracelessly with embarrassment and manoeuvred myself backstage. But the incident imprinted the power of words on my consciousness.

Mrs Wise Replies

I also played parts in Eily McAdam's historical plays which gave their first roles to schoolboys, including Milo O'Shea and Eamon Andrews, who came straight from Synge Street Christian Brothers School to act in them. Although I too had acted in her plays I didn't meet Eily until 1938 when, having completed the course at the Abbey School of Acting, I started work as an editorial assistant on the fortnightly women's magazine, *Woman's Life*, which she edited. She was thoroughly professional, having learnt the business on a Donegal newspaper owned by her father. Eily McAdam was a tiny little woman from Donegal with a mop of silver hair and a permanent interrogative look in her bright blue

Three generations at Clonliffe Road. Back row: Michael Horgan (Nina's husband), Kevin, James, me, Harry, Phauds, Jack. Middle row: Molly, Mother, Father, Nina, with Denis on her knee. Front: Michael and Anne Horgan .

eyes. She smoked non-stop but everyone smoked in those days.

She taught me everything she thought I ought to know to enable me to counter the onslaughts of the advertising manager who had a habit of bursting into the editorial department (one room which I shared with Eily) demanding 'puffs' for this or that product. I enraged him by adamantly refusing to 'write up' such things as certain patent medicines which I knew to be useless. He once accused me of introducing filthy sex into the magazine when I wrote a piece about a new restaurant which had had a gala opening. I praised its summery decor and its salad bar, an innovation novel to Dublin. I mentioned that it was attracting a happy young clientele. Some were holding hands. *In public!* That poor man, the father of twelve, gave Eily and me many a good laugh.

One of my duties was to conduct the 'Mrs Wise Replies' column. The letters addressed to this Mrs Wise were written in hope of genuine helpful advice. The majority of problems fell into one of three categories: loneliness, blackheads, and accidental pregnancies. Advice on blackheads was easy. Loneliness far more complicated. Pregnancies were a serious matter sometimes demanding further confidential information and permitted consultation with qualified agencies. Tragedy lurked.

Much as I liked working with Eily I didn't really see myself in the role of agony aunt. Checking knitting instructions for garments from an Aran sweater to a lacy bed-jacket was another incompatible chore. And sorting photographs of competitors in the Swan Beauty Competition was a blind alley, especially as I suspected that it had nothing at all to do with celebrating the beauty of Irishwomen but was designed to sell Swan Beauty products. Competition was intense. The winner was promised £50, a week's stage engagement, and a film test with the implication of film stardom.

I hated the whole business. Up and down the country decent young girls spent good money on studio photographs for which they'd dressed elaborately and had their heads tortured to show off hair stylists' skills. Mothers and aunts 'phoned, wrote and called to the office in attempts to influence judgement. Those determined enough to call must have been surprised to meet little Eily, sucking away at her fag and with several pencils protruding from her bush of hair; and to see me, behind a huge old typewriter, irritably tapping out captions for pictures of unlikely winners. They left with Eily's assurance, uncomforting as it was, delivered in her strong Donegal accent, that the judging committee was absolutely independent.

The winner, a lovely, charming girl, had been chosen before the competition was even announced and had no part in the charade. She was the inevitable target of the press photographers at the Grand Ball for the beauties in the Gresham Hotel when the finalists were presented and the winner announced. I was appointed to do a running commentary of the event on radio for which I got no fee and so felt at liberty to say what I pleased. I rattled on at the microphone, conventionally enough, until Eily caught my eye and winked.

She covered her face with her beaded reticule when I launched into a description of her distinguished inimitable style, her crown of silver hair and her brilliance as the editor of *your* magazine, *Woman's Life*. The last reference was inspired to assuage the fury of the committee. If the venom they directed at me could kill I should not have lived to boost the product but it did mollify them a little

This was the highlight of *Woman's Life* for 1938. St Valentine's Day of 1939 called for a special edition devoted to love. One of us found an old, creased article in a drawer which fitted the bill. We designed different layouts and decided on a border of cavorting cupids which considerably enhanced the innocuous text. The piece was unsigned. It was so old that it hadn't occurred to us to identify the author. She identified herself, a Miss Y, fiftyish, not someone identifiable with St Valentine, the patron of romance.

She wanted her fee, five guineas, no less, when most writers were satisfied with one-and-a-half, at the most three, and she decided to sue the magazine. The directors decided to fight the case. They spied publicity. Headlines.

ELDERLY SPINSTER AUTHORITY ON LOVE.

SPINSTER SUES FOR LOVE.

WHAT PRICE LOVE IN A WOMAN'S LIFE?

The assistant editor knew all the journalists in town. The directors reasoned that if she gave evidence for the magazine in court the press would be sure to attend and get a great story out of the case. What matter if it cost a few bob? The publicity would be invaluable; but the assistant editor had also been thinking that Eily and she weren't paid half enough for what they did for the magazine. The article wasn't great but the woman had written it. She should be treated with respect. It wasn't up to me to make a fool of her. If the directors thought I'd set her up they had another think coming.

I stood in the witness box and swore to tell the truth.

'And what are your wages?' Miss Y's counsel asked in a contemptuous tone.

'Wages!' I was incredulous. 'Need I answer the question, my Lord? I think it is impertinent.'

'It is somewhat . . . No, you need not answer it.' The counsel didn't know that I knew the District Justice quite well and the fact that he was hearing the case gave me the confidence to speak up.

No, I had not known who wrote the article. Yes, we should have tried to find out. No, it was not necessarily the custom to return unused material to authors. Yes, of course, once the material is used it must be paid for. No. I didn't think a fee of five guineas was exorbitant. After all the author hadn't had the use of her money all this time.

She got her fee and her costs. It was time for me to say goodbye to Eily and concentrate on acting and scriptwriting.

Mena at war

In September 1939 war was declared. A line in a letter from Mena in Leeds mentioned a rehearsal for an air-raid. Mena, by now a Sister with specialist training in neuro-surgery, was invited to join a mobile neuro-surgical unit designed to research and treat head and brain injuries in the battle areas. The idea for such a unit had been conceived by Hugh Cairns, surgeon-in-chief of the Radcliffe Infirmary in Oxford. Mena, now a member of the Queen Alexandra Imperial Military Nursing Service, left for France with the team on 13 May 1940 as German forces began to encircle Belgium. After three days driving through the battle zone, they reached the casualty clearing station near Lille at midnight. They started work the next day and had to operate on the basis of first come, first served with emphasis on cases capable of surviving. There were few head injuries but other casualties came in droves. Conditions were chaotic, a complete muddle. Orders to pack and evacuate were cancelled only to be repeated within the hour. On 20 May, just four days after their arrival, they were finally ordered to pack and to wait for further orders. Two days later they set out for Belgium and arrived in their lorries at a convent school-cum-hospital in a village called Krouhelse. Terrified refugees, with English and French soldiers in retreat, crowded the hospital and stretched all staff to the limit.

On the morning of 29 May, only sixteen days after leaving England, the women staff were ordered to leave immediately and to take only what they could carry. They had to do the unthinkable: down tools and leave eight hundred patients to the mercy of the approaching Germans. The team of doctors opted to stay with their patients even though they could do little to help them. With other nurses from other clearing stations Mena and her assistant packed into an ambulance and were driven hell-for-leather through unimaginable confusion, caused as much by the retreating army as by despairing civilians, to La Panne, near Dunkirk. The tide was out and the mine-sweeper, HMS *Oriel*, which was to take them off, was beached. After seven hours of bombing, causing damage but making no direct hit, they got under way and even-

Cheered by troops at La Panne, near Dunkirk, Mena (centre) and friends boarding the HMS Oriel, *with 'only what they could carry'*

tually arrived at Harwich, hungry, dirty, shocked and exhausted. The doctors were captured eighteen hours after the nurses' departure and put to work in hospitals at Ypres and Étaples.

Mother and I had been glued to the wireless listening to every bulletin giving news of the defeat of France and telling each other that it didn't matter if she came home without an arm or a leg so long as she came home alive. When she did come home on leave, Mena was unnaturally quiet in herself. She did not talk of her, so far, short war experiences. One day, as we sat round the table at lunch, it was announced on the wireless that the *Royal Oak*, a British warship, had gone down with all hands. Mena put her hands to her face and abruptly left the table. She lay on her bed for hours, weeping uncontrollably. It was as if a pent-up torrent of grief had been released and overcame her. Some of her medical associates had been on the warship.

At last she forced herself to read a letter from Oxford delivered some weeks before. It was from Hugh Cairns. He was now the Nuffield Professor of Surgery in the Radcliffe Infirmary and Surgeon-in-Charge of St Hugh's, the College which had been turned into a military hospital for head injuries. He asked her to write a detailed account of her experiences from the moment of going into action. She was almost speechless with fury at the many stupidities she had encountered. Where to begin? I suggested it would be easier in the detachment of a formal report so one sunny day, we sat in a bushy corner of the garden and she began to write. I helped by taking her day by day through the twenty-two she had spent with Neuro-Surgical Unit No.1. Her criticisms of the ineptness of the expedition were legion.

She was not particularly enamoured of Dublin, either, which she found poverty-stricken, spiv-ridden, spied in and spied on, shamelessly black marketeering, irredeemably frivolous. There were certainly some strange characters around—Herbie, for example, an American. There was something a little mysterious about him, He came to Dublin to go to Trinity but to what purpose he never said and learning seemed to be the last thing on his mind. He seemed to have loads of money. He lived in an apartment in a converted coach-house in a laneway off Baggot Street, newly christened Dublin's Left Bank. He gave parties which lasted for days. Friends, acquaintances and total strangers wandered in and out of them at will. Herbie welcomed them all.

He would indicate loaves of bread, a slab of butter, a chunk of cheese and a large coffee pot. If someone brought a bottle of wine or a few bottles of beer or stout they were instantly shared. Poor Herbie was not much to look at. He was flabby rather than fat with a complexion on which a breeze had never blown; of a colour which we attributed to central heating, an American luxury we had heard about but never experienced. The backs of his small white hands were covered with black hair.

Was he a spy? A draft dodger? Some people briefly speculated but his open door disarmed suspicion. He talked books ad nauseam and was finally accepted as a literary nut-case with a romantic notion that Dublin was the only source of anything worth reading.

Then there was the curious encounter with David Levi. He was a mature student at Trinity, a champion squash-player, Herbie told me. I met him when I went to his apartment with two friends to deliver text-books they had promised to lend him. He insisted on making coffee and produced exquisite Swiss liqueur chocolates to eat with it. Chocolate of any kind was a dreamt-of luxury because of rationing and we enjoyed several of these, restrained from scoffing the lot only by David's air of familiarity with a surfeit of such goodies.

David's acquaintances tended, in his presence, to acquire a sophisticated manner to match his imagined expectations so when he put on a record of a Mozart concerto I sat back to listen attentively as if Mozart was my usual night-cap. When my friends rose to go, mumbling an excuse about early lectures, I groped for my handbag. David handed it to me but asked if *I* had to go. Would

I not hear the concerto out with him? So much more enjoyable in company. The friends urged me to stay and quickly abandoned me to Mozart and the athletic David.

We sat in silence until the record came to a standstill and David began to talk of his love of opera and of how Dublin was starved of it. I sat thinking of the only time I had seen opera; it was in Belfast when an extremely fat soprano sang the word 'love' drawn out and contracted, up and down the scale an unnecessary number of times. So I was startled when David said, distinctly, 'I would love to marry you'. To his credit he did not say 'I love you', only that he would love to marry me.

'Gracious!' I cried. 'Why on earth . . . ?'

'I have an uncle in Argentina. He owns thousands of acres. He wants me to go there. The life is good. Think of riding the pampas in the early morning! My uncle would choose a horse for you. He'd have it broken in and trained just for you.'

My brain spun. What do they call cowboys in Argentina? What would they think of David, whose face, I noticed for the first time, was powdered? Did he hope to disguise his colour, a delicate tan, or was it just an affectation? Perhaps he was as good a rider as he was a squash player. After all, Arabs are said to be marvellous horsemen and I had assumed, since meeting him, that he came from somewhere in the Middle-East. Why me? A wife to impress his uncle? To gain Irish citizenship? A passport? Any woman would do.

'Think about it,' he pleaded.

'No, David. You think about it. I can't help you but it was nice to be asked. And thank you for a lovely evening.'

I was quite sincere in my thanks and left serene and unmolested. I hope he found someone to ride out with him in Argentina, someone who appreciates opera.

Heini was a German, a journalist stranded in Dublin when the war started. He was blue-eyed, blond, handsome. The German

Party time! Molly is on the left, Nina is just behind Lord Mayor Alfie Byrne, and Basil is beside Nina

ministry appointed him Press Officer 'for the duration' that is, in an honorary post until the war ended, which added prestige to his attributes. He had the glamour of foreignness and a supremely confident manner. I was present once when he banged a café table with his fist to emphasise his opinion of what could be done with Ireland with strong management.

He was friendly with a journalist on one of our national news-papers, a young man who greatly admired Hitler's organisational talents. He had come home from a holiday in Germany in a long trench coat worn with a military air. He took Heini under his wing and introduced him to his circle and it was no surprise that Maria attracted his attention. She had been to Paris to do a course in Cordon Bleu cookery and had acquired a chic dress-sense, sim-plicity itself, which set off her trim figure. Her black hair, bobbed and fringed, was a perfect foil for his blond head, all the more so since her height matched his.

The term 'boy-friend' was not then in common use but all of us assumed that he was her man. He gave a party for her birthday in his apartment. I was more than taken aback to be asked to admire his presents to her, black lacy underwear displayed on a table. Maria was nonchalant on a sofa, demure in a short navy dress with white Peter Pan collar and a silver cross hanging from a silver chain. Her long legs, in enviable, rare, silk stockings, were entities almost separate from her body so blatantly they were displayed.

Heini chose a record and a couple started to Charleston. Someone asked me to dance and as we kicked sidewards and slapped our knees I noticed the door of a corner cupboard partly hidden by my gyrating partner. When the music stopped I leaned against it while I recovered my breath. A scene was painted on the door in heavy impasto. There were holes, about the circumference of a pencil, bored at intervals through the wood. Without thinking, I opened the door to have a look. I had barely time to see some sort of machine when the door was pushed closed and Heini told me in a cold and even tone that supper was ready in the next room.

'I'm sorry, Heini,' I said. 'If curiosity really killed the cat I should have died a hundred times by now,' and, confronted by a table covered with Cordon Bleu food and bottles of wine, I forgot the incident.

I remembered it when one afternoon, two or three days after Mena returned from France, I answered the doorbell to find Heini before me. I hadn't seen him since the birthday party, but had heard rumours about him. He was a spy. He was a Nazi. He was a propagandist. It could be that he was just desperately anxious to know what was happening at the front for he must have been frustrated and worried about his own people.

It was a lovely day but, even so, I was amazed when he asked me to go for a swim. I politely refused. My sister had just come from France. She was exhausted. She needed to rest.

'Oh, bring her along,' he urged. 'A swim would do her good.'

'But Heini,' and I think I sounded shocked, if not pompous. 'You're *German*. She couldn't possibly go.'

He looked at the ground for a moment, then turned sharply

and left. As he had almost certainly been followed by a Special Branch detective, it was just as well that his visit was short and that he left alone.

Herbie, the American, was still with us. His sister arrived one day and I saw the flicker of annoyance that crossed his face as he tried to greet her with some degree of enthusiasm. A studious looking young woman, she wore heavy horn-rimmed glasses and a long, droopy, hand-knitted coat. She had been sent to try to persuade Herbie to go home to New York. He had been forgiven, she told us, though not for what.

She said that *she* thought his poetry was very good and that if he worked harder at it he could make a fortune writing rhymes for Christmas cards. Herbie looked thoughtful with a more positive expression than I'd yet seen on his face. Stubborn. One of the party people, obviously rent by curiosity, invited the sister to go with her to a café for tea. The others drifted away, propelled by a slight embarrassment, while Mona Blair-White and I stayed on, as we usually did, to tidy Herbie's kitchen up a bit as a sort of 'Thank you' for the party.

Herbie went upstairs and we heard him moving about. The noise of his steps on the wooden floor sounded purposeful. We saw that he had a suitcase in each hand when he came down and stood at the kitchen door.

'We'll meet again, don't know where, don't know when,' he quoted from a popular song and smiled at us. '"S been great knowin' ya,' he said and left.

We never saw him again. It was a relief not to know where he had gone, that he had not given us an address or a telephone number. His sister hung around for a week or two, hoping he would turn up, I suppose. We heard years afterwards in the way things come round in chance conversations, that he had gone to Canada, edited for a while for a publishing company and quietly drank himself to death. There was no news of the sister. 'Poor

Herbie.' 'So decent.' 'Harmless.' 'A really nice man.' 'So misunderstood.'

They were strange times.

Hugh Cairn's letter and a reference to her captured colleagues had galvanised Mena into action. Along with her report she posted an application for inclusion in a new team then being formed. She wanted to carry on the work and to put her experience at the service of the first team's successors. Besides, she missed the camaraderie of team effort, the feeling of belonging and the sense of being in place, a necessary cog. She left Dublin to join Neuro-Surgical Unit No. 2 in July, 1940. Censorship cut direct communication but news of her, sometimes at second or third hand, was relayed through a network of well-wishers. It was some time before we learned that she was bound for the Middle East. She left Oxford on 4 May 1941. On the first evening out the ship hit a submerged wreck and had to turn back on a slow frustrating limp up to Glasgow and down to Liverpool where they were told to take two weeks leave while the ship was being repaired. This homecoming was almost humiliating, an anti-climax after her arrival of the year before; and we were preoccupied by the bombing of Belfast in April and again in May which had brought the war horribly close. We hated the thought of her involvement.

Thirteen people died and Short and Harland's fuselage factory was burned out in a raid on the night of 8 April 1941. It was nothing to what happened on the nights of 15/16 April. Waves of German planes rained obliteration on streets of little houses where dockers and their families lived. Affluent houses in the Cave Hill and Antrim Road areas were hit. Explosives meant for industrial targets made dust and ashes of the houses and the people in them while more accurate targeting destroyed factories, shipyards, electricity and water supplies.

Seven hundred and forty-five people died in the five hours the raid lasted. Thousands fled into the country to shelter where they

In the drawing-room at Clonliffe Road

might, many walking for miles for want of transport as petrol was severely rationed. Shortly after midnight on 4 May the Luftwaffe returned and bombed hundreds of acres of works and workers' homes into a sea of fire.

Molly was living and working in Belfast. Luckily, she had been having dinner with friends on the night of the big raid, for a bomb blast had all but demolished the house in which she rented a flat. She was now staying with an old friend from Coalisland, Dr Evelyn McDaniel, and Mena decided to go to see her before her leave expired. While Mena went to Belfast I got on with the inevitable shuffling and making of beds in preparation for an influx of Molly's friends who needed, she said, a day or two to get over 'it'.

I hoped they would bring some food with them. Would they eat parsnip tart? Parsnips were supposed to taste like bananas. It took ages to sieve the coarse, blackish, war-time 'flour' through a silk stocking to produce enough relatively white stuff to make a cake or pastry. Gas for cooking was allowed for limited periods three times a day. In between, it was possible to steal a flicker from the jets to boil water for a cup of tea in defiance of the dreaded 'glimmer-man' who had authority to enter houses to track down law-breakers and had mythical powers to punish. In fact, all he could do was to threaten a summons.

'Make do and mend' was the order of the day in Ireland as in

England. Shortages tested ingenuity to the limit. Ordinary personal and household things disappeared from the shops and improvising replacements took time and effort. We mended ladders in stockings, darned holes in the heels of socks, joined the edges of sheets worn or torn in the middle, saved slivers of soap to boil together to use for washing clothes. We wasted nothing and economized in a way undreamt of in today's domestic practice when planned obsolescence reigns.

Mena badly needed a new stock of underwear. Our combined ration coupons were not nearly enough to exchange for the necessary garments even if we could find them made from natural fibres which mother insisted were obligatory next the skin in hot climates. When Mena and I failed in a search Mother said, 'We'll try Clery's.' If she could wheedle some stuff from the man in 'dress materials' she would make the things herself.

A bolt of fine cambric was the only suitable material Clery's had. It was lavender coloured, not white. 'A pity,' she told the assistant, 'but it'll have to do.' She charmed it from him and bore the whole bolt home. Panties, camisoles, petticoats and pyjamas piled up to the whirr of the sewing machine. A princess couldn't have commanded a prettier trousseau, we told her, nor would it be made with more care. (Sad to say, it proved irresistible to others. As Mena travelled about and had no way of securing her property it slowly melted away, abstracted piece by piece).

Her longed-for call to arms came at last and we left her to the boat for Holyhead.

Joe does his bit

Brother Joe had also been in uniform and was soon in a position to be more saluted to than saluting. He had joined the army volunteer reserve established by de Valera in 1933 to block the activities of the Blueshirts. The volunteers wore a grey uniform with forest green trimming and German surplus stock coal scuttle helmets. It was a natural progression in patriotism for him to volunteer for the regular army in 1940 when The Emergency was declared. Since the country was officially neutral in the war against Germany his safety was reasonably secure. Though the training was very tough he enjoyed the mixed company and the unlikely pickles he found himself in.

Training started in a temporary barracks in part of St. Mary's Hospital in the salubrious Phoenix Park and continued in the Arcadia Ballroom in Bray. There he slept on a bed of three planks covered by a thin mattress raised a few inches from the ground. He couldn't do much harm on thirteen shillings and two pence a week so when he got a chance to do a Potential Officer's Course at the Curragh Camp on the plain of Kildare to study for an examination in 'the language' he took it, and got it, with elevation to the rank of 2nd Lieutenant.

Having been awarded the Fáinne, a badge signifying the wearer's ability to speak Irish, army logic dictated his despatch to the élite Irish-speaking 1st Battalion in Galway, known to other units as 'the Tá Sés.' He found the Fáinne less than helpful in the task of explaining the intricacies of the rifle, the grenade and the Lewis machine gun to native Irish-speaking recruits from the Connemara Gaeltacht and applied for a transfer. He was posted to the 17th Infantry Battalion in Donegal and slotted smoothly into the Vickers Machine Gun Company under the command of Joe Gilroy, a fellow Tyrone man from Omagh.

The nearest he got to active service was sitting in a lorry one

Joe

night, armed to the teeth as he told it, ready to take on the British, German and American armies should any of them attempt to invade our dear native land. An exploit, of which he is still proud, was walking (he could have said marching—it would have sounded more military—but he didn't) from Donegal to Cork and finishing in a wade across an icy river at dawn.

He was further promoted to the rank of 1st Lieutenant. As such he was in great demand at céilidhs and dances with opportunities *go leor* to exercise his charm, greatly matured since he exercised it on the Misses McCann in Dungannon so long ago. How they would love to have a photograph I have of him, immaculate in his uniform, shoes shined and laces tied. They would think it worth much more than thixpence, but would hardly dare to ask for kisses.

Part 3 Gaps of brightness

'For to articulate sweet sounds together
Is to work harder than all these, and yet
Be thought an idler by the noisy set
Of bankers, schoolmasters, and clergymen
The martyrs call the world.'

(from 'Adam's Curse', W. B. Yeats)

I WAS BEING REGULARLY INVITED by Radio Eireann to contribute
to talk shows and to perform in a variety of productions. The
poet Roibeárd Ó Faracháin (Robert Farren) was Talks Officer and,
happily, was in a position to promote 'the word' in spoken verse
and in verse plays. One evening in 1939 when, after performing in
Lennox Robinson's radio production of Yeats's play, *The Green
Helmet,* I walked down the long corridor of the Station with him,
I remarked that verse-plays, especially when choral speaking was
concerned, should have a great deal more rehearsal than ordinary
plays. He suggested further discussion, approached his friend, the
poet Austin Clarke, and The Dublin Verse-speaking Society was
formed. Its inaugural meeting was held on 6 December 1939 at 5
Leinster Street. Austin became Chairman, Roibeard Vice-Chair-
man. I was invited to be Hon. Secretary and Eve Watkinson, the
actress, Hon. Treasurer. The other founding members were Wilfred
Brambell, Brian Carey, Nora Davies, Margaret Griffith, Deirdre

Broadcasting with the Dublin Verse-Speaking
Society with (standing, left to right) Robert Mooney,
Eithne Dunne, Ruaidhri Roberts, Lawrence Elyan,
Florence Lynch and (seated) Austin Clarke

Halligan, Cecil Jeffares, Florence Lynch, Donagh MacDonagh, John O'Gorman and Madeleine Reeves. Members over the years included Eithne Dunne, Maureen Kiely (who married Cyril Cusack), Ronnie Masterson, Dan O'Herlihy and Liam Redmond. Gordon Bottomley's dictum 'the sound of poetry is part of its meaning' became the Society's slogan.

We met regularly for rehearsal at various venues and often at the Clarke home, Bridge House in Templeogue. Austin's wife Nora distributed our scripts to us and 'sat in' as we rehearsed in the book-filled sitting-room. We gave poetry recitals in the Abbey and Peacock theatres; and recitals for special occasions such as a dinner in November 1941 to welcome the poet, Joseph Campbell, on his return from America. Over twenty-five years, our voices became familiar to listeners country-wide through Radio Eireann's Monday evening poetry programmes, introduced by Austin, and annual Christmas Eve programmes which included translations from the Irish of old Christmas poems.

Nowadays poets (and others writers) often read their own work at readings or on radio and, it must be said, not all of them read well. The reading of poetry depends on trust in the poet's words, each chosen to express exact meaning; the quality and control of the speaker's voice (*not* accent); and a capacity to enter into the spirit of the poem. It is not easy and it requires hard practice, enough to unselfconsciously *possess* the poem, even to ecstasy.

At the time the Dublin Verse-speaking Society was set up rural culture and customs had become the fashion, fostered by the Abbey. Born and bred urbanites cultivated the 'brogue' to exemplify their integrity as the genuine article in Irishness. When Yeats recorded his best known poem, 'The Lake Isle of Inisfree', he spoke in an execrable imitation of a country brogue. It was the height of praise to say of anyone that his or her accent hadn't changed 'since the day he or she left home' when in such cases all it meant was that he or she had no 'ear' or for political or other reasons wanted to distance themselves from people tinged with Anglo coloration. Austin Clarke did not change his own mellifluous middle-class Dublin accent. Our approach was well understood by *The Irish Times* of December 1940: 'Their voices are clear,—every vowel and consonant are there, with nothing slurred: they are cultivated voices—"cultured" if you insist—but every one of them has its own personality.' ('The Irishman's Diary')

The personality identification was borne out years later by a couple standing at the bar in the Great Southern Railway Hotel in Galway. The barman had refused to cash a cheque for me and I had to get to Dublin in a hurry.

'We'll change your cheque if you like,' the young woman said to me and her companion nodded in agreement

'But you don't know me,' I answered, surprised.

'But we know your voice,' she assured me. 'We always listen to the poetry programme on Mondays.'

That voice must have had something distinctive about it for it got me a husband.

'He has a motor!'

Early in 1941 Austin Clarke asked me to read 'The Three-Cornered Field' by F. R. Higgins for a Radio Eireann live broadcast:

By a field of the crabtrees my love and I were walking
And talking most sweetly to each other;
In the three-cornered field, we walked in early autumn,
And these were the words of my lover:

'A poor scholar like me who never took to girling
Finds book-knowledge such a bitter morsel—
Yet were I a clergyman, wise in holy learning,
O I'd make your wild beauty my gospel.'

And softly, softly, his words were moving through me—
Coaxing as a fife, crying like a fiddle—
That I heard my heart beat, as dew beat on the stubble;
And the twilight was then lying with us.

In that three-cornered field, while the moon was whitely
   filling
The grass there gave hunger to our passion,
And so said my love: 'With the New Year, let me give
   you
The red marriage ring for a hansel.'

Since then I never hear him, but soon O I'll see him
Just darken God's doorway on a Sunday—
Yes, darken God's doorway as he darkened my reason
And narrowed my daylight last summer.

So again by the crab-trees, the grass is lean with autumn
Where again I'll be waiting for my lover;

And while he'll never know it, with him I'll go walking
Although he is wed to another.

A senior Radio Eireann administration officer heard it and
decided that he must meet the speaker whose identity he thought
he knew. He wrote a polite note and invited her to meet him for
dinner, or the theatre, or something—I never learned what. She
wasn't the person he had thought she was. He tried again, nothing if not persistent.

Being of senior rank, at a time when seniority counted, he was
able to infiltrate a short rehearsal before a performance and, by
devious means, he identified the reader, this time correctly. He
waited for the programme to finish and sequestered me from the
group as we left the studio. We walked down the corridor together chatting amiably and said good-night as the rest of the
readers caught up with us. A note from him two days later suggested that I give him the pleasure of my company at the first
night of *Rebecca,* a play from the novel by Daphne du Maurier. I
was happy to go, not least because Rupert Strong, poet, journalist
and editor, had commissioned me to interview Hazel Malcolm,
the leading lady, for his magazine and I was glad of a chance to
see her perform. I accepted the invitation with a vague image of a
tall, extremely good-looking man in my head.

'He has a motor!' Mother laughed delightedly as, from the
window, she saw him pull up at the gate. She was fed up seeing
me escorted home by two portly producers, Jack Stephenson and
Gabriel Fallon, a printer and civil servant, middle-aged married
men who shared the productions of Eily McAdam's and other
one-act radio plays. I never knew, nor asked, why they bothered
to see me home. Then there was the penniless medical student in
his third final (!) year whose idea of a night out was going to the
pictures and a bar of chocolate. The poor fellow nearly frightened
the life out of me by taking me to meet his widowed father at
their home in one of 'the roads' in the district which is now known
as Dublin 4. He suggested that if I could put up a thousand

pounds he would marry me. He got short shrift and that was the end of him.

If this new fellow had a motor . . . ? I could see Mother calculating. On the way up Grafton Street to the Gaiety Theatre, a woman, without a look to right or left, walked off the pavement and fell on the road right in front of us. In a moment my escort had helped her to her feet and brushed her down. She assured him that she was perfectly all right, thank you, there was no need for a fuss, and sauntered off, quite unconcerned. She had taken no names or numbers and, satisfied that she had come to no harm, we proceeded.

We had plenty to say to each other and several more meetings were necessary to say more; but the next time we went out he arrived by bus and by bus we went to the cinema.

'No car,' I commented.

'I sold it.'

'Why?'

'I'm saving up to get married.'

'Oh?'

We married in September. Mrs Henry Boylan. Me!

It was partly thanks to Molly, that we did marry in September as arranged. My brother Daniel, the second eldest and third child in the family, had died in August after a short illness. He was forty-three. I thought we should postpone the wedding. 'No,' said Molly. 'Get married now or you'll end up as the girl at home.' She and her friend, Mai Geldorf, took care of the preparations in which poor Mother took little part. But she made my wedding dress of pale lilac moiré silk, and made it exquisitely.

We spent our two weeks' honeymoon in Portnablagh in Donegal. The hotel was an old house modernised and extended and managed by Dermot Walshe. We soon realised that we were in a dream dreamed by millions who would never share our luck. We spent our days walking on long wave-washed beaches. We hoiked huge crabs out of cracks in the rocks when the tide went out and

*Our wedding. Joe Boylan is to Harry's right, Father and
Mother are just behind us and Molly is to my left.*

brought them back to the hotel to be cooked for lunch or dinner.
I paddled at the water's edge while Harry ducked and dived through
the spume.

We hired bicycles and explored the area for pagan carvings and
examples of ogham writing on ancient stones. We dawdled along
and stopped often to listen to as well as look for the falls and
rushes of little streams over rocky beds making music to accom-
pany the blowing clouds chasing against distant hills and throw-
ing shadows on the coloured land. We gathered blackberries and
enjoyed them later cooked with apples in tarts. We ate of the
produce of two acres of kitchen garden, as if possessed by hunger
demons.

Quantities of scallops, big fat mussels, turbot, lobster, all kinds
of fish were brought straight from the wild waters of the Atlantic

Off on our honeymoon

and entered the hotel menu according to the catch of the day. Lazy and sated we'd sit in the drawing room and talk until dark. One evening a guest wished that Portnablagh had a picture house. A soft northern voice, slow and persuasive, informed her:

'There's a travelling company coming to do *Julius Caesar* on Saturday night over in Carrigart. I was told they were very good.'

We introduced ourselves to the speaker and asked her if she'd like to come with us to the show. Her name was Ulrica Donnell. She had lived in Strabane with her widower father until he recently died. She was now at a loss to know what to do with her time. We urged her to go to Dublin. Study. Do a course. She'd be sure to find something to suit her. We gave her our address and invited her to look us up if she did come. One Sunday morning as we came down the aisle in Donnybrook Church after Mass we came upon her leaning against the wall, looking out for us. She was studying to be a lady almoner (or medical social worker) at Trinity College. She became a friend for life.

We had rented a top floor flat on Merrion Road for £90 a year. It had a large sitting-room, a dining-room, kitchen, bathroom, and two bedrooms, one large, one small. We covered the floors with Belgian hair-cord carpet which was cheap and durable and we scoured secondhand shops and auction-rooms for furniture. I got to know the quays intimately and made friends with interesting and knowledgeable characters along the way.

Our view from the windows of our flat was of sky so that I often felt I was on a ship as clouds sailed by and seagulls flew from nearby Sandymount Strand to the Royal Dublin Society's buildings, across the road, to pick up spilled grain from feed for the horses stabled there. In summertime we watched, from our balcony, the gallant women of inner Dublin pushing prams full of babies and toddlers with bigger children holding the hands of little ones, or clinging to their mothers' skirts, heading for the sea. And, in the evening, we watched the tired procession on its way home. The young ones held up sun-burned arms and begged to be carried. Mothers scolded, pleaded, promised 'it wasn't far now.' They'd soon be home.

My admiration of those women in those hard times was total. Rationing, of even such things as soap, was just another penance to endure added to their problems of daily struggle. If they could fit in a bit of an outing for their families and themselves they never missed an opportunity. They had a talent for enjoyment and they used it.

Family matters

I felt as I imagined a film star must feel as I sat up in bed in a bower of flowers in the Leinster Nursing Home, in Pembroke Street, with Hugo, our newborn baby, perfect and beautiful, by my side. Harry was ecstatic. He couldn't wait, he said, for the day they'd go together for a pint. The Leinster was an up-market home, really beyond our means.

A coal fire burned in the grate of my large private room. Antique furniture was more decorative than useful. As I luxuriated in an ambience of carefree comfort, pampered by family, friends and nurse, I reflected that a purpose-built modern home would be altogether more efficient, economical and hygienic. When crises occurred in nursing homes patients had to be transferred to major hospitals where expertise in the different areas, and facilities for dealing with them, were concentrated. It seemed to me, as an SRN, that to go to hospital in the first place was the sensible course, but our income was just above the maximum allowed for admission to the National Maternity Hospital, my preference if I'd been allowed one.

Most families in our situation employed domestic help and we engaged a maid-of-all-work at the going rate of eight shillings a week, and a sewing woman who came once a month to turn collars and cuffs, to patch and darn as was required. Bridie, our live-in help, was from a remote townland in County Kerry. Her work, so far, was undemanding as I did the cooking and the washing went to a laundry. It was delivered on Saturday afternoons in two parcels, Finished and Household. Bridie was a devout Catholic. She adored the baby and would have given up her half-day to play with him if I hadn't insisted that she needed to get out of the house, in reality to give me a chance to play with him myself. We were blessed, we agreed, to have such a good girl to help us for without her I couldn't have kept on writing and broadcasting.

We assumed that the girls she met on Saturday nights to go to a dance hall were as good and religious as she was. 'Jalousie, ma'm, Jalousie . . . ' When she came home she'd sing, with a rapt look on her face, the words of a popular song, *Jealousy*, as she whirled around the kitchen to demonstrate how she had enjoyed herself. When she urged me to go to confession on Saturdays, because that was the day the Canon 'heard' and he was a 'lovely man', I left the house and went my nefarious way until enough time had passed for her to think that I had been shriven, paid my penance

Baby Hugo on the musnud

and prayed. By the time I returned the laundry man had been and gone.

Hugo's arrival dictated a move. Carrying his pram up two flights of stairs to our flat at the top of the house was a chore too many. Besides, he was an extraordinarily alert infant and it was obvious that he would soon need space to exercise his exploratory instincts. At the age of ten months he astonished us by creeping after a ball and walking with it from under the table, babbling delightedly. Bridie came with us to Dundrum in 1943. We rented, at £120 a year, the half of a large Georgian house, Annaville House. Our part included a half-acre fruit and vegetable garden, a hen house, and a potting shed. Our neighbours commanded a paddock in front and two groves of trees. One of them was on a mound which became a desert island, a fairy fort, a foreign country, a ship, as the fancy took the children. It was an idyllic playground for the children's early years.

Bridie worked like a beaver helping us to settle in. Furniture had to be bought. We had notions and wanted nothing ordinary. No three-piece suite for us! I remember a musnud, a sofa of oriental design with curved ends and round cushions fitting into them, made to order for us by Millar and Beatty in Grafton Street. The salesman must have smiled behind his hand as he listened respectfully to our instructions. Two armchairs with upholstery matching the musnud's were made to measure, the smaller with high back and draught-excluder sides for me and a big, deep, well padded one for 'sir'. Lawler Briscoe on the Quays made two mahogany single beds with fretted head and footboards at £50 for the two for the spare room. We picked tables, chairs, cupboards, even pots and pans and other sundries from secondhand shops.

Bridie was in her element. She took it for granted that she should climb ladders to hang curtains. She scrubbed and sandpapered and painted in a fever of enthusiasm while keeping the baby in sight. She explained to him what she was doing and he followed her every movement with inquisitive eyes. 'Mind that now for I don't want to have to tell ye twist,' she'd admonish him.

One day was particularly busy. I stayed at home because of my interesting condition while Harry represented us at the wedding of a friend. We expected some of his fellow guests to come back with him for supper. Sometime in the afternoon Ulrica Donnell arrived unexpectedly on her bicycle. I was glad to see her for she was the one person we could depend on to take us as she found us. She joined me in the kitchen while I fiddled around preparing the supper. There was a loud knock on the door and a confusion of voices. Ulrica followed me out in time to help a man to support my father into the sitting room.

The man looked frightened and Father looked ghastly for he was ill with chronic anaemia and under doctor's care. Today, of all days, he had decided to visit our 'estate', as he jokingly called it, and in appropriate style. He came in a horse-drawn cab from O'Connell Street. The bump and rattle all the way out to Dundrum nearly did for him. Ulrica and the relieved cab driver laid him on the musnud. I fetched brandy. The baby began to cry and Bridie came in to say she had a terrible headache and she'd have to lie down. 'Do! Bridie, do! Go and have a good rest. I'll bring you a cup of tea and some aspirin in a minute,' I told her with more than a touch of asperity. What a time for her to have a headache!

My exasperation was exacerbated by my father's evident enjoyment of the brandy. Ulrica had quelled Hugo's yells which had subsided to heart-broken sobs when we heard a roar from on high. 'I'd better get that tea and aspirin up to Bridie,' I said to Ulrica and nodded significantly at Father on the musnud meaning that he should have no more stimulant. One red eye was all I could see of Bridie's face buried in the pillow. I told her to take the aspirin and drink the tea while it was hot and that I'd come up again shortly. There was plenty of tea left in the pot so Ulrica and I sat

Harry with Hugo in the garden at
Annaville House

at the kitchen table to drink a cup and to plot Father's safe return journey.

I invited the cab-driver to join us and he agreed that the poor old gentleman would be better off to get home quickly by motor for the horse, champion though he was, could do no better than four miles an hour. I paid him and he promised to call to the hackney driver in Milltown and to ask him to come as soon as possible. While I dealt with him I was sure I heard another roar, but smothered, from upstairs. That girl, I thought crossly. No restraint. Can she have taken the aspirin at all? I chose to ignore her and went in to have a look at the poor old gentleman. He was comfortably asleep, snug under Harry's Crombie and looking all the better for being a little flushed.

Hugo was happy playing in his pram with a rag book. All was peaceful and quiet; but Harry and our guests were soon due. Food was more or less ready but the table had to be set, Hugo bathed and put in his cot, the fire lit and Father taken care of. If the hackney didn't come I'd have to keep him for the night. Maybe Bridie was feeling better and would be down to help? An unmerciful yell dispelled such optimism. Father sat up, startled. Ulrica spoke slowly and calmly, saying: 'Those noises sound very rhythmical to me. I think we'd better get a doctor,' and without more ado she went to the door, mounted her bicycle, and sped down the driveway to the doctor's house adjacent to our gate. He stood at her bedroom door and looked in at Bridie.

'Better get an ambulance. Get her to Holles Street straightaway.'

'Holles Street!' I was outraged. 'You haven't even looked at her. She's a good religious girl. She could have *anything* wrong with her.'

'She could indeed. Ah, Mrs Boylan, have sense. I'll see about an ambulance. Pack her bag and waste no time,' he ordered and left.

Bridie clung to me, implored me not to send her away, she'd

swear on her bended knees, she'd be no trouble. She wept hysteri-
cally as I put her night things into a suitcase, adding toiletries of
my own. 'Poor Bridie,' I kept saying soothingly, foolishly. How
could I keep her? I'd be gone myself any day now. The master
would have to take time off to look after the baby. The thought of
'the master' in charge quieted her and, sullen and angry, she sub-
mitted to being dressed.

The simultaneous arrival of the ambulance and the hackney
was a bonus. Father, who looked to be a likely candidate, de-
murred at being put into the ambulance. The hackney looked
askance at the teary stout country girl whom Ulrica was gently
coaxing away from his cab. They got into the ambulance together.
She knew the drill, Ulrica said. She'd see me tomorrow. The hackney driver and father sailed off in the cab. 'Poor Bridie,' I said to
Hugo as I carried him upstairs for his bath. 'Poor, poor Bridie.'
He patted my cheek and I'd swear he looked sympathetic.

Our new girl, Mary, was a foster child of a wonderful woman
from the Dublin hills who trotted up the avenue one day in her
pony and trap to show her new foster-baby, a boy, to Mary and
us. From her sympathetic description of 'the poor young one'
from Kerry with relevant dates and details, by an extraordinary
coincidence the mother could only be Bridie. Harry had got her a
place with his sister Kitty but heavy make-up, bleached hair, scarlet nails, stiletto heels and late nights were all too indicative of
trouble ahead. Anyhow, Bridie told a relieved Kitty when she gave
notice to quit, Blackrock was far too far away from the town. So
she passed from our ken while I had plenty to think about.

Dr Tim Healy was a charmer. He gave the impression of having all the time in the world. You were his only patient. I aired my
idea of an ideal home to him when for some reason he booked me
into Hatch Street (equal in status to the Leinster and just as old-
fashioned) for the birth of our second treasure, Anna. It would be
a great boon to thousands of women like me, who were neither
rich nor poor, if he and his colleagues would get together and

build a nursing home based on function, I suggested. All we needed was a bed, a table, chairs, in a well-lit airy room with a bathroom en suite. In those days a week, or even two, were allowed for the birth and recovery. No one needed the trimmings of the current arrangements for such a short time. I assured him that women would flock to such a home.

A bit characterless? Not at all. There'd be flowers and family photographs to liven up the room. The new baby would be the centre of attention. Who'd even notice the décor? He smiled benignly. There'd be difficulties. Y'see, we're not businessmen. A pity. A patient in 'the Hatch' was obliged to engage her personal nurse. One of her duties was to queue every morning for hot water drawn into a large enamel jug from a communal cistern and to carry it downstairs for her patient's toilet.

My nurse was cheerful and caring but she did harass me sometimes into buying silk stockings or Swiss soap, which I neither needed nor could afford. She was going to Grafton Street. She had heard that Switzers had silk stockings and God knows when they'd get any in again. I'd be foolish to miss the chance of a couple of pairs and, sure, it was no trouble to her to get them for me when she was getting some for herself. I succumbed to the stockings and the soap and other small things she suggested. An item on her bill was puzzling. Porterage? What was that? Oh, that was for doing my messages. And so one lived and learned.

News from Cairo

Meanwhile, letters from Mena in Cairo had informed us that she had been billeted in the 15th Scottish Hospital at Giza on the main road to Mena Camp and the pyramids. It was staffed by the Aberdeen Royal Infirmary and the Royal Infirmary, Edinburgh. It was new and up-to-date and fully equipped. The operating theatres were 'the surgeons' delight' with shower-rooms and restrooms en suite.

Mena in the desert with Neuro-Surgical Unit No. 2 medical team

The nurses' living quarters were three house-boats laid end-to-end on the Nile. Food, was 'plentiful'. Figs, pomegranates, apricots, oranges, lemons, water-melons, peaches and mangoes were commonplace. She loved, 'above all, a ripe, juicy mango.' (The nearest I came to an orange was a thick concentrate of orange juice in small bottles, strictly reserved for pregnant women and babies.) Nurses had the run of the Gezira Club which was an island in the middle of the Nile. A boatman ferried them to it whenever they wished. Officers of the Allied Forces were made honorary members for the duration of the war. Acres of green lawns, a swimming pool, tennis courts, a golf-course and polo ground were at their disposal.

The nurses had an open invitation to dinner dances in the officers' mess. At the end of an evening when one of Mena's partners had repeatedly asked her to dance, 'it seemed natural that he should escort me back to my house-boat'. This was Francis Devereaux Lambert who became her husband. He called a taxi, left her at the gangway, called 'Goodnight', and departed the next day for Beirut where he served as a public relations officer attached to General Spear's Mission headquarters.

Public school in England, followed by a year each in France and Germany, designed to prepare for a career in banking, equipped

Mena and Fran outside Annaville House

Fran equally well for service with the Mission. His father lived on an income from a family trust derived from the Harrison Shipping Company, Liverpool. Fran persuaded Mena that as 'anything' could happen they should marry and fixed the date for the 18th of January 1943. Mena had not dreamt that she would ever marry a man who was not an Irish Catholic and who was unknown to her devoted family. Fran was a stickler for protocol. He asked her permission to write to our father to ask *his* permission to ask her to marry him. Father was already aghast at what she was up to but she knew that his sense of humour would be tickled by Fran's formality. His reply was solemn and determinedly Victorian in tone. The words 'honour' and 'trust' were invoked but he stopped short at mention of 'his little girl.' (Mena was thirty by this time.) Fran was impressed and couldn't understand why Mena laughed. The important thing was that Father wished them well and Mother sent her fondest love since there was nothing else she could do.

It was what was known in Ireland as a mixed marriage, as he was Church of England and she was Roman Catholic, 'a second-class affair in the eyes of my church, even in war-time, even in Cairo so far from home'. There were no flowers on the side-altar of the Military Chapel in the hospital. Music? No. She wore uniform and carried a bouquet of roses and felt, she said, 'faintly bridal'. The celebrant, Father Jackson, an American padre, told her that she didn't have to be too strict about her promise to honour and obey. They spent their wedding night in a hotel in Cairo and next morning they parted to take up their separate duties but they did have a honeymoon in Beirut two weeks later.

By the time the British and American forces had brought the Western desert war to an end. Mena was on her way home having taken a distracted leave of her husband. He survived, physically unscathed, in the fleshpots of Beirut.

Dublin, with its bright lights, was another world. The family was, of course, delighted to have her back but apart from catching up on family news, she was hardly with us. She was edgy and spent her time walking the streets, getting her bearings and generally sorting herself out. And she had the pleasure of meeting my husband and of seeing us settled, for the present anyhow, in a home of our own whereas we had not met Fran and she was a transient, unsure of her next assignment. She was furious to learn that our letters to her, even our love and good wishes for her wedding day, had been returned to us. And she was furious all over again as she denounced the stupidities of war. 'No wonder morale was so often at rock bottom among the fighting men.'

When Fran came to Dublin for the birth of his son, it was obvious that he was uneasy and at a loss. He and Mena and baby John came to stay with us in Annaville House and were with us

Harry and I in front of Annaville House with Hugo and Anna

for some months while my sister tried gently to wean him from a gentleman's expectation of cooked breakfast, morning coffee, light lunch, afternoon tea and evening dinner. He was agreeable enough but could be taciturn and we agreed that it was hard for him to adjust to a peace-time of persistent shortages. He was good with his baby son. He took him for walks in his pram and seemed not to notice the stares of passing men who thought that pushing a pram was a sissy thing to do.

He would have liked to settle in Dublin given acceptable conditions. These were not available to him, any more than to the many Irish returnees jostling for position, who as natives had the advantage of fighting familiar corners.

Part of his work on General Spear's staff was in public relations, which he thought might give him an entree to journalism. I invited a journalist friend to dinner to give him an idea of local newspapers' requirements. He didn't connect and we spent the evening talking around him in the hope that he would pick up some useful pointers.

Brother Phauds had become something of an entrepreneur and, for Mena's sake, was willing to turn over a branch of his business to Fran. Preliminary discussion made it clear that Fran's goal was partnership and, as Phaud's ego was just as imperious as his, the deal fell through. It had become evident that the want of a specific qualification and practical experience in the real world would take time to overcome. He came and went between Dublin and London and started and stopped in a number of trial runs until he finally left, after just three years of marriage, leaving Mena to return to nursing, to live in the family home in Clonliffe Road and to bring up their infant son alone.

Father died at home, just before Christmas 1946, aged seventy-seven. That winter, and the spring of 1947, were the hardest for decades. Ice and snow lasted until May. Keeping the children warm was a major problem. Layers of woollies were a help, but didn't stop Hugo, now attending a local kindergarten, and Anna, a two-year-old toddler, from getting painful chilblains. I remember myself, walking from Dundrum down the middle of a glassy road between piled up dirty snow, a freezing wind at my back, crying with the pain of the cold.

I set out for the broadcasting station one day. The car slid down the hill in Milltown, out of control, and it was a miracle that it didn't crash before the wheels got purchase on the main road into town. By the time I got to Henry Street my legs, frozen with the cold, felt like tree trunks and I had difficulty getting out of the car.

Harvesting

Nature's inexorable cycle began again with the spring. Most of Europe had been wrecked by the war. Cultivation of crops had come to a full stop in many places. Recovery was slow and available food had to be diverted to starving survivors living among the ruins of lost homes and bomb-pocked lands. It behoved the lucky ones, we were told, to make ourselves as self-sufficient as possible. The fruit trees and bushes were well established so that we had as many eating and cooking apples, pears and plums, as any family could possibly need. We were self-sufficient in vegetables too. There was plenty to spare and it was pleasant to be flaithiúlach with produce fresh from the garden. Nothing happens by magic, of course. There was a great deal of labour in keeping diseases at bay, pruning, feeding, spraying, weeding, mulching and harvesting.

The loganberries were luscious but it was purgatory gathering them for tiny red mites defended them and we'd end up with as many bites as berries. The gooseberries were torture to get at. We often felt inclined to leave them to rot but, next to blackcurrants, they're the easiest of all fruit to make into jam and there's no nicer summer dessert than cool, pale green, tart gooseberry fool. There were times when we'd have loved to give the lot away but relations and friends shied from the thorny job of picking them. It was easier to barter them for a pound of this or a dozen of that with our grocer for he'd send his boy to pick them.

It was the same with the tomatoes that grew in the old broken-down greenhouse. It accommodated a hundred and twenty plants. It was another world in there, steamy with heat and quiet as a chapel. The lovely pungent smell clung as we went about the callus-making job of tying up the heavy trusses and nicking off side-shoots. It was tiring work but the taste of a tomato fresh from the stem made it well worthwhile. Neighbours used to come to the door to buy a pound or two; but they'd haggle over the price, low as it was, even with the few extra thrown in for luck, and the chat took an awful lot of time so the tomatoes were bartered as well.

When the apples ripened they had to be sorted, the best kept for storing, individually wrapped and laid on the shelves in the potting shed. It was a relief to close the door on them. All we had to do now was to sweep up the leaves, put them on the compost heap and forget about the garden in the few weeks of the dead of winter.

Every weekend husbands, fathers and capable sons disappeared to adjacent boglands to cut turf for family fires. Electricity and gas were still in short supply long after the war ended and wet turf was a poor substitute for coal. So were the logs sawed from branches of trees by Harry, lost in the leaves and precariously balanced on an old ladder steadied by me.

It was hard, time-consuming work and getting the logs to burn required patience and ingenuity. I spent hours scraping ends of candles on to sheets of newspapers, rolling them and twisting them into knots to make beds for the logs and, hopefully, to generate enough heat to dry and ignite them. It is hard, now, to imagine the amount of labour engaged in the simplest task for want of ready fuel but it seems to me that we enjoyed the challenges. Every problem overcome was a huge satisfaction.

The empty hen house was a daily accusation. If we had our own eggs I wouldn't have to wheedle an occasional extra few from our grocer. As if we hadn't enough to do we washed down the hen house with disinfectant and laid out two runs for alternate use. We took advice and were told that White Sussex were good layers. We bought twelve and the deliveryman turned them, shrieking with malice, from a small wire cage. They were beautiful but fierce. They balefully inspected their quarters.

Neighbours and relatives flooded me with advice. They also loaded me with rejects from their kitchens. If hens liked yellowing cabbage leaves, stale bread and potato peelings what they fancied should have done them good. 'But don't overfeed them or they'll get too lazy to lay,' the neighbours warned. Sensibly, the hens supplemented their diet with every blade of grass in their alternating runs in double quick time. They pounded about in mud and dust in frantic worm-hunting sorties.

Some took to squalling at each other while others let themselves go and sat about in despondent squalor. They did lay eggs—now and again. They weren't eggs as we know them. Most were misshapen. Some of the shells were almost transparent. They barely held the contents from oozing out. Some were eaten by the hens for cannibalism was not the least of the flock's disgusting habits.

They pecked each other viciously and I sighed in despair when yet another bald pate displayed itself.

Everyone waited for the day when they would share my 'natural' eggs. 'Free-range' had not yet entered shoppers' vocabulary; but it was a time when government help was at hand. The Department of Agriculture would send an expert, free of charge, to advise the grower of the smallest of crops or producer of eggs, as in my case. Ashamed of my failure, I rang the Department for help.

The poultry instructress arrived in a blizzard one spring morning. I led her to the hen-run. Her face was a study of compassion as she scooped up the nearest bedraggled specimen and clasped it to her heart. It was clear that she had a passion for hens. 'Feel that,' she said, directing my reluctant hand to the bird's wet crop. 'It's empty,' she accused, not looking at me, and clucking tenderly over the dirty feathers. Gently, she laid the hen in the shelter of the hen-house door.

'We'll go in,' she said, slapping the snow off her hooded coat. She sat in silence while I made tea. I poured it and sat opposite to her, a penitent waiting for sentence. She coldly gave me a run-down of food values contained in an egg.

'And how do you imagine that all of that is going to come out in the egg if it didn't go in the feed?' she asked.

Humbly I wrote down the scientifically balanced diet she prescribed. I had often passed the Blanchardstown Mills shop on the main street in Dundrum and I was delighted to have an excuse to go into it for it was to there the Instructor directed me. I bought layers' mash, oyster grit, and, I think, Indian corn, or was it some sort of coarse oats? Anyhow, I scattered some oyster grit in the hen runs and put some out in an old tin basin. I cooked big feeds of layers' mash mixed with some of the neighbours' scraps for the birds and threw them a fresh green cabbage to tear at.

In no time at all the hens were glossy and plump, cawking-cawking away to each other like happy gossips and producing almost more large, strong-shelled eggs than I could cope with. I told the neighbours about the new scientific diet, that I didn't need the scraps. Of course I gave them eggs when I had any left from our own and Mother's supply. It never seemed to occur to them that they were costing me, never mind the cooking of the feeds, the care of the hen-runs and the daily clean out of the hen house. We were so lucky! It was well for us! And we were. And it was.

The ducks defeated me. There was a fairly deep depression, a sort of cement basin under the tap in the yard. I thought it would be just about big enough to keep a couple of ducks happy. I was seduced by a poem by F. W. Harvey in which he calls ducks 'soothey things'. It begins:

> From troubles of the world I turn to ducks
> Beautiful comical things
> Their heads beneath white wings
> by waters cool . . .

and it goes on in a very sentimental and deceptive manner.

The children would love the ducks. They would make pets of them. They would be their responsibility and they would learn a lot. They could use the stiff brush to scrub the basin every day and fill it with fresh water from the tap. That was my optimistic thinking on a lovely summer's day and things might have turned out differently if Sweeney and Todd had been normal but these ducks were distinctly peculiar.

They paid not the slightest attention to the water and they menaced the children with long unblinking stares from their beady eyes. They became perfect pests. The kitchen door opened into the yard and I dreaded having to open it for the charming pair had invariably taken up their station outside and would fall over their feet to get in and do their best to trip me up with their waddling this way and that way. They followed me everywhere, serenading me with a duet of raucous quacks. It wasn't that they were hungry. You just couldn't fill them. And they were dirty—

droppings all over the place. In fact, they were noisy, greedy, demanding, filthy beasts and we could see that all the good will in the world would never change them.

They had to go. With mixed feelings of guilt and regret we tricked them into a sack. Hugo and Anna were very quiet in the back of the car, fearful that the ducks might escape from the boot, but we got them safely to the zoo. We released them near a pond where a variety of duck species was disporting. It was magical. They sailed away, all grace and dignity. They turned over and waggled their tails as if in derision. They were comical all right. We laughed and Hugo and Anna clapped their hands.

My sister-in-law, May, was preparing to open a maternity nursing home in partnership with a friend, Nan. On the day, the house was not quite ready to receive patients and Kato had, perforce, to make her entry into the world in her own time and in her own home, well assisted by Nan. I had all the care and comfort needed to make it a happy experience in my self-absorbed cocoon. I was totally oblivious of family and household disruption. Hugo and Anna had to subdue their enthusiasm for the baby whom they were allowed to hold for only a minute and certainly not to carry out to show to the hens.

Their visits to the bedroom were strictly regulated and it became evident that they would blame their little sister for keeping me upstairs when they had been assured that there was nothing wrong with me. Their father acquired a wan expression which said louder than words that the sooner things returned to normal the better. Nan was marvellous. Of course she was. But was it fair to keep her from other patients? Fortunately, Kato 'bloomed like a tulip' as our friend and neighbour, May Jordan, enthused and she was brought downstairs to take her chances.

Peter timed his arrival better; the new nursing home was successfully up and running. May and Nan were immensely proud of this new baby who was just as beautiful as his brother and sisters. Hugo and Anna were old enough to be excited on their first visit to meet him. Anna even claimed him as she climbed on to the bed and clamoured, 'S'mine! S'mine!' We brought him home on a sunny day in July. The orchard was frothing with blossom. The girls clung to my skirt. Hugo put his hand in Harry's and Harry put his arm across my shoulder and slowly we walked under the trees and felt an intensity of emotion we knew to be happiness.

Little hero

A family holiday on a farm in Wexford was not a happy one and was memorable for its abrupt end. The weather was lovely. There was a splendid beach with safe swimming nearby. The farmer and his wife joined us for superb home-cooked, home-produced meals. Their little girl, their only child, Sarah, soon overcame her shyness. It was natural that we should invite her to come with us when we picnicked on the beach and to share in the children's games. The trouble was that she didn't know how to play. She couldn't swim and her idea of fun, for example, was to throw spadesful of sand over our lot when they came, dripping, out of the sea.

One of them lent her a bucket to make turrets for a sandcastle they were concentrating on building. Hugo had collected a little mound of shells he intended for decorative touches on the castle. It was between him and Sarah as we sat in a circle to eat our lunch for which her mother had kindly given us slices of her new-made spongy soda bread and hard-boiled free-range eggs. Sarah didn't want any. She said she'd wait for the lemonade and chocolate biscuits we allowed as a holiday treat. It was plain that she was impatient but I thought it best to treat her as I would one of my own if he or she was being tiresome. And was Sarah tiresome! We made excuses for her. She was only five. The poor thing had no one to play with. She wasn't used to other children.

There was suppressed violence in the way she played with the shells. She'd pick up a handful and dash them down again as if wanting to break them. While I watched, right under my eyes, she delicately picked out a piece of broken scallop shell and deliberately threw it up at Hugo. Of course she didn't aim it at his eyes but it did penetrate his left pupil and stuck there. Harry picked him up in his arms and shocked and speechless we made for the farmhouse to pack.

It's so hard to remember the sequence of events in such circumstances. I do remember that Hugo was admitted without delay to the Eye and Ear Hospital in Adelaide Road. We took him for tea to the Country Shop on Stephen's Green on the way and bought him a wooden toy. A Sister received us at the door of the ward and we delivered our son to her. In those days parents were not allowed to stay in the hospital with their children. Hand-in-hand Sister led him away from us. Half way up the ward Hugo looked back. My pain was physical, unimaginable. What went on in his head? Did he think we had abandoned him? What could we do? Rules were rules.

The consultant, Dr McAreavey, operated on him the following morning. The prognosis was that the child might lose sight in the affected eye but there was hope that it might be only moderately affected. This didn't alter the fact that poor Hugo was in the dark, his eyes bandaged, for a week or more. I can't remember for how long. I do remember that the nurses called him a hero. They fussed over him and petted him and restored him to us as brave and uncomplaining as he had been from the moment of the accident. Some people urged us to take an action against the farmer. To make money out of our son's and his daughter's misfortune? It was not an option and we were grateful to have him home with us, very little the worse for wear.

We had to attend Dr McAreavey's clinic at the hospital for regular checks. Time went on and we began to fret about the potential size of the consultant's bill which we expected to be astronomical and wanted to provide for so that we could pay it promptly. After many visits and the kindest of attention I at last rang Dr McAreavey's rooms and asked his secretary to arrange for a business meeting with the doctor.

I was diffident, not sure how to broach the matter.

'We were wondering, Doctor. We haven't had a bill from you yet and we thought it might have got lost in the post or something.'

'Bill? Bill? What bill? I know nothing about a bill.'

'For Hugo,' I faltered. 'For the operation and the treatment and everything. It must be time you were paid. I've brought a little instalment,' and I took an envelope out of my bag.

'Look,' he said. 'There you were, a young couple starting out in life, enjoying a holiday when that happened to that wonderful little boy of yours. Forget about bills.'

I began to cry.

'Well now,' he said gruffly, 'if you really want to get rid of your money, give me that. I'll give it to my wife to buy herself a hat. That'll please her and it'll please me if you'll forget about any old bill. Isn't it great that Hugo's doing so well?' and he rang the bell for his secretary to come and see me out.

Our first house

Four children, twelve hens, a sometimes absent husband, responsibilities towards parents and siblings and writing commitments dictated drastic reorganisation. Harry had moved from Radio Eireann to mainstream civil service duties and his increasing workload was reflected in neglect of the garden. We did have the help of a wonderful neighbouring man who came to us when his arthritis allowed him to work but as stiffness and pain took hold we accepted his need for retirement. It hurt to leave Dundrum but we were a family now. It was time to secure a future, to buy a property of our own, for paying rent, we solemnly agreed, was money down the drain.

Housing, then as now, was in short supply. The government offered grants to first-time buyers. The same buyers suspected the builders of adding the grants to the price of the houses thus negating the benefit to them. The grant itself had a price. It circumscribed the size of the house which, on paper, seemed to be reasonably generous. 'Estates' became a feature of urban planning and no attempt at disguise by giving them names with connotations of baronial grandeur or of rural promise could hide their boring sameness. Our house was in Churchtown, the one and only one on the site when we bought it in the early 1950s. Sheep grazed around it. We convinced ourselves that our choice was a good one. Soon, however, we were surrounded by identical dwellings and lines of washing flapping in the wind. Our next-door neighbours, whom other neighbours had christened Navy and Black, had no children and were irked by ours who missed the freedom and space of Dundrum and couldn't understand the constraints of living at close quarters with such grumps.

We nicknamed the neighbours who were opposite in every respect to Navy and Black, The Opposites, also because they lived opposite to us. They were an altogether more uninhibited pair. They dearly loved a party, two of which passed into local folklore. One was given by them; husband and wife failed to consult each other and each, in biblical mode, went out into the highways and byways and invited every friend and acquaintance. Crowds turned up, far too many to be accommodated in the house. No problem. The dining table was upended and brought out to the front garden. Volunteers rushed away to procure more food. Others washed plates and forks in relays. Glasses were exchanged. Bottles were circulated. Music. Must have music. Six stalwarts heaved the piano to the middle of the road. It was a balmy night and song serenaded the stars till the early hours.

The second party was to celebrate Hallowe'en. The husband Opposite said it was to be fancy-dress. We said it wasn't. His wife agreed with us. We were spoil-sports. He would go as Louis Armstrong whom he revered. He polished his face and neck and hands and bald head with black Nugget shoe-polish. He rubbed it well in and he did, indeed, look a little like the great jazzman.

He was the only one in fancy-dress. Everyone took their cue from the hostess who thought she was being tactful in pretending not to notice Opposite's plight. They all started to talk very loudly. 'Silly sods,' his wife said to me. 'I'm going home,' so we left without speaking to any of them. It took a full week for the Opposites to get rid of the polish. In spite of massage with cold cream, olive oil, thick pastes of flour and shaving cream and steaming, the Nugget, like a bad cold, ran its mottled course, until the last traces behind his ears and at the hairline framing his head finally faded away.

Going west

We loved to go west in the summertime and took to renting a house somewhere in Connemara for four weeks during the children's holidays from school. I shudder now to think of the long journey sitting in the front of the car with the baby on my lap, without benefit of safety belt, over winding, pot-holed, rocky roads. But then, because the roads were so bad, there was no possibility of speeding and courtesy was imposed by necessity.

We packed clothes, sometimes bed linen as well, into a huge laundry basket and sent it ahead by rail for delivery to our house. We had to pack for every climatic eventuality. Even so, we were defeated once when it rained so incessantly that we gave up and came home a week before time. That disaster was balanced by the month when it rained the day we arrived and the day we left, with sunshine and bliss every day in between. In other years the weather gave us its usual mix of wind and calm, sunshine and showers. It dictated our activities.

The house we rented for that particular idyllic month of July

Cavorting on a beach

was near Cleggan. It was set on a grassy hill frilled with lacy walls. We climbed over a stile to reach a deep well of clear cold water, cleanly lined with whitewashed stones. A stream of bog-brown water made music as it rushed down the hill through gulleys and fell over rocks then disappeared into the cavernous ground under a great slab of slate from Clare, beside the gate. Watercress grew on its banks and wild thyme and myrtle scented the air as we crushed them on our first tour of inspection. Later we found wild strawberries, the tiny, juicy, perfumed ones that gourmets pay fortunes for.

The children pressed close to us in silent delight at sight of a donkey standing still beside a rain-barrel at the gable end of the house. Smoke curling from the chimney was no surprise for this wouldn't be the first time we were welcomed to the west. Sure enough, we saw through the open door the fire on the hearth, the table set for tea with eggs in a dish and a big bowl of scones. We'd been watched for. Settling in is a private business, Mrs O'Flaherty, our neighbour and caretaker of the house, told us when she called in the morning.

We had brought books on wild-flowers, birds, shells and fish and she was able to put Irish on most of their names. Hugo led the hunt for specimens to keep in a mini-museum. A small bird's perfect skeleton, a saucer-full of shells, a goat's skull found in a hedge, wild flowers pressed in books of blotting paper, a piece of glittering mica, oddly twisted pieces of dried sea-rod, bulrushes in a stone beer-bottle, a ball of sheep's wool gathered from bushes, bits of driftwood—these were enough for an exhibition proudly displayed and endlessly rearranged.

To this day I use two sea-rounded stones brought from the beach. I use them to press boiled tongue, to tenderise meat, to keep a lid on a pot, to crush garlic or grind black peppers or to crack walnuts. Every time I take one in my hand I hear bog water rushing and smell wild thyme. I can taste the mackerel fresh from the sea that kindly Pat O'Flaherty caught from his curragh. I can feel warm sand through my toes and I see the heat-haze veiling the distant hills that summer.

The widow O'Flaherty lived nearby with her three young daughters. Her fingers did a neat little set-dance along the needles as she knitted and talked. If she wasn't knitting she was footing turf, or making hay or churning at her door. The girls lit the fire for me. They took the bucket out of my hand if I needed to go to the well for water; and they taught us to set-dance so as not to make fools of ourselves when we went to their house for a céilí. They pleaded to mind little Kato, whom they called 'the young one', and baby Peter. One day I packed the seven children into the car and went for a drive on the long lick of land, Streamstown, that tongued its way into the inlet from the sea.

The road was springy, being built on bog, and soon it sagged and billowed like a feather mattress. If we climbed a rise and sighted the sea the children shrieked as we seemed about to slither into the blue. Finally, I saw that there was no going forward and how was I to turn back? But butterflies flickered over flower heads, iridescent dragonflies hovered and spiralled and birds swooped high and low. The sun shone, the sea and the sky were blue, there was a smell of new mown hay and it seemed that we were stuck in paradise. A short reconnoitre found me a gap in a hedge. I backed into it and with difficulty managed to get out again, pointed in the right direction and, with fervent 'Thanks be to Gods' from the widow's girls, made for home.

A farmer came to the door one day hand-in-hand with Hugo who was clutching a water-lily. The little wretch was clearly enjoying the drama. The man looked at me with angry contempt.

'The child might have drowned in the lake above,' he said. 'It was the mercy of God that the greyhound bitch escaped me and I looking for her in a place I don't often be at this time of the day and I to see the child over the water on a rotten stump of a tree.'

My eyes filled with tears for I saw in the beautiful pale waxiness of the waterlily the imagined drowned face of my son. But: 'Come on,' ordered the man. 'I'll show you a bit of foreshore that the cattle don't trample.' And so it was that we had the run of a perfect small beach, floored with clean silver sand, enclosed by a cave-riddled cliff.

Another holiday, this time in Co. Kerry with children and grand-children, was memorable for tragedy averted. We had gone to the strand at Cloghane. The tide was out and from where we sat on the rocks was a tidy distance from the sea's edge, just far enough for a walk, a bit of exercise. Róisín, my granddaughter, aged ten, offered to come with me. We scolded about a helicopter bussing low over the strand,, that it flew too low, that we couldn't hear ourselves speak with the noise it made.

We passed a couple of small children splashing on the slope of a deep pool which seemed to have been scooped from the beach by something like an excavator. It was wide, the sides shallow enough; but I wondered and was uneasy about its depth. The helicopter was a distraction as it rattled, higher, away into the distance. It left an unnatural quiet as if ordinary sounds had given up competing with it. And then we heard the children screaming.

'Those kids are having a great time,' I said hesitantly.

'Grannie! They sound panicky.'

We ran back to the pool and, as she ran, Roisín pulled her tee-shirt from over her swimsuit and threw it to me. The boy was thrashing the water desperately trying to hold his sister who seemed to have gone limp. Now, without energy to shout, he piteously rasped meaningless sounds. Roisín said nothing. She just dived in and swam. She lifted the girl's head above water and kicked her way to where I, halfway down the slope, dragged the child from her while she swam back and supported the boy with one arm as she encouraged him to make it to the side.

I had turned the little girl on her front and had set to pressing water out of her lungs. She took deep sobbing breaths and very quickly sat up and began to cry. By now Roisín had calmly collected the children' clothes and bundled them neatly together in the boy's shirt. She shook their towels and, in her friendly, smiling way, she draped them round their shoulders. She took the girl's hand and we followed the boy, running ahead, to where their parents sat, unconcernedly reading. I must have been in a mild state of shock for I didn't speak to them. Roisín laid the clothes on the sand beside them leaving the children to tell, or not, of their adventure.

The time we rented Arland Ussher's house in Carraroe, years before Róisín was born, stays in our minds because Brendan Behan spent a day with us there. Harry had gone to the shop to get milk for the breakfast. We had begun to think he'd gone for good when he arrived with Brendan in tow. He was en route to the Aran Islands, to Inismore I think, to write a book but was not, apparently, in a great hurry to get there. The children loved him. He was shy and concentrated on talking to them, easily and naturally, when he wasn't talking in Irish to Harry whom he called Einri.

We drank mugs of tea and he was pleased and impressed that the soda bread we ate in thick slices was made by me in the pot-oven. He stayed by the fire in the kitchen telling the children stories which widened their eyes in disbelief and made them laugh. He watched me cope with a couple of lobsters bought at the back door at two shillings and sixpence each from Paud who had hauled them up in his pots only an hour before. Brendan was a knowledgeable gourmet. He greatly appreciated fresh lobster freshly cooked. He nodded approvingly as I made authentic mayonnaise with egg yolks and olive oil, subtled with the crushed half of a clove of garlic.

Then we went to the beach. The men went for a swim. We sat on a low wall and watched Brendan cavorting like a dolphin and joking with the small crowd of locals and holiday people who had gathered to see our celebrity. They responded warmly to his nonsense and would, I hope, think kindly of him later when sycophants exploited the generous extrovert side of his nature and egged him on to drink and destroy himself. We had the lobster with the mayonnaise and wheaten pot bread with apples and cheese after lunch. Brendan wasn't drinking so we all drank water and Einri left him back to his lodgings.

Then there was the month we spent in Tully when Anna developed an affinity with Peter Nee's Connemara pony and ambled on it, bare-backed, up and down the road and on the beach along the water's edge. Kato and Peter were happy to toddle along beside them until they got bored and abruptly stopped to make a sandcastle or to search for jetsam entangled in seaweed cast up by the tide.

Peter Nee was a gentleman who sold us legs of tender Connemara lamb for next to nothing. An English friend and his Australian wife, Noel, came to stay with us. She and I lay on a big flat rock taking the sun one day. We heard Peter whistling to his dog as it rounded up his sheep on the hill above us. The barking of the dog, the whistling and the baaing of the sheep emphasised the sense of utter peace. Presently the dog trotted past us and, without stopping or giving us a glance, Peter laid a bunch of wild mint beside me and continued on his way. A bouquet of red roses wouldn't have been more welcome! Noel exclaimed: 'Where else on earth . . . ?' I knew what she meant.

A fine solid little pier ran down to an idle little harbour in Tully. Barbecue was not a word then known to us, but, in effect, we often enjoyed barbecued lunches on that pier. A large biscuit tin with a row of holes punched around its base, with the grill from the house gas-cooker on top, made an excellent cooker. Tightly rolled up newspaper, twigs and scraps of dried sea-rods fuelled it. Lamb chops, lightly charred on the grill and pink in the middle, couldn't have been more delicious, eaten with Kerr Pinks boiled in their skins and brought down in an enamel basin from the house. Pudding could be anything from pieces of chocolate to fruit or slabs of buttered brack.

Now and again Harry and I took off on our own to do some quick shopping or to explore possible new sites for picnicking. Next to Clifden, Roundstone was the nearest sizeable town to the village of Ballyconneely. One year we rented a house in the area and made Roundstone our metropolis. If you stand on the quay and look across to the Twelve Bens you'll see a small island, Inislachan, lying to the south some miles out to sea. Sometimes it disappears in mist or rain or heat-haze but we always looked for it and it became an obsession, as islands do.

One blazing day we hired a rowing boat and pulled away from the quayside. The sea was flat calm. It was almost sinister out in the bay for great patches of absolutely still black water denied us buoyancy and it was hard work rowing so that I imagined we might make no headway, be caught forever there or find ourselves in a whirlpool, sucked down and down, cold fathoms deep. But as our oars broke the surface and silkily stippled our wake so we broke the distance and, at last, glided into clear shallow water gently rippling over a bed of golden sand.

A wide arc of beach shelved down to meet us. The sand was warm to our bare feet as we hauled the boat above the tide line. The silence was total. No sign of human habitation marked the beach. I felt our presence there to be an intrusion. The beauty of the place was thrilling: the sea and the sand and the sky; the trees sculpted by the wind into heroic shapes and the cubist mass of a building against the skyline looked as if painted by a master artist. We ran to explore, zig-zagging up the beach.

The building was a schoolhouse, built in 1850, a stone in the lintel told us, but it was a long time deserted for all the furniture was gone and fallen plaster strewed the floors. Is there anything so sad as a deserted schoolhouse? We turned away and started to walk along a grass track that led inland through hedges tangled with brambles and spicy with the scent of honeysuckle. I stopped suddenly and my husband whistled for he had seen what I saw. A thin question mark of smoke wavered in the air ahead of us. We hurried towards it.

It came from the chimney of a thatched cottage sinking into the ground by the side of the track. The whistle had roused a dog. It ran from side to side of the open gate, barking furiously. It circled us as if we were sheep and prevented us from moving either backwards or forwards, then bounded to the gateway again as if daring us to approach, then back to circle us again, snarling and panic-stricken. And then the woman called him. She came to the gate and fondled his head.

It's very odd but I can't remember what she looked like, except that she was old, maybe not as old as she looked. My eyes were on the dog. It had relaxed but was still tense and ready. The woman was neither friendly, nor unfriendly, just noncommittal. 'Yes. I am the only one on the island. No. I am not Irish. Yorkshire. Good dog. It's all right now.'

She had no curiosity about us. She just waited for us to go as if we were disturbers of her private peace. From Roundstone we looked back at the island, now more mysterious than ever. Every time we go through Roundstone I look over to it and wonder why a woman from Yorkshire should live there all alone.

An opened door

After only a few years our house in Churchtown began to silt up with our own and the children's possessions. The paraphernalia of study and leisure were all over the place. Hugo's, Anna's and Kato's bicycles and Peter's tricycle were awkward things to store and it was a nuisance having to put away my typewriter and the old Singer sewing machine every time I used them. Harry's papers and books kept crowding precious shelf space; but moving was out of the question.

We were too busy, anyhow, to bother about small inconveniences. We would organise things better when we had time. That time eluded us for Harry developed a condition which necessitated a minor operation and a ten-day stay in Mount Carmel Hospital, in Rathgar. After a few days he was allowed to go out with me for short walks. A *For Sale* notice on a large, red brick Victorian house attracted our attention and the invalid thought to relieve the boredom of his ordered regime by having a look at it. Mrs Bell, whose house it was, opened a small glass screen be-

15 Orwell Park

hind an ornate grill let into the door, and examined us. She opened the door and invited us in.

She was so gracious that we backed away explaining that there was little chance of our buying her house, that we wouldn't want to waste her time, that we were just curious.

'Come on in and have a look anyway, now that you've got this far.' she insisted.

She pointed out all the things that would need to be done, mainly in the area of redecorating. Wrinkled brown paint covered the solid pine panelled doors. The majestic bath in the room at the top of the house had a few rust spots. We told her they could easily be treated and pointed out that the bath was an antique and valuable. We exclaimed over the six bright bedrooms, each with a wash-hand basin and a gas fire.

'I'd get rid of that,' she said, as if advising us, pointing to the stone sink crammed behind the kitchen door.

The kitchen would never feature in a glossy magazine but it was a model a woman could swear by. The window looked on to a long wide garden, a Bramley apple tree in the middle of the lawn. The wall facing it had a built-in dresser hung with mugs and jugs, its shelves displaying plates and dishes. Its cupboards housed a variety of every necessary cooking utensil. A door gave access to a cellar to which coal was delivered via a hatch in the garage. A long scrubbed table with drawers at each end, which Mrs. Bell said had been a tailor's cutting table, stood in the middle of the quarry-tiled floor. I imagined myself making an apple tart at one end of it while the older children at the other end did their homework and Peter played underneath, like Joe and Bridget in the long ago. An Esse cooker gave out a gentle heat and promised twenty-four hour service as Mrs Bell demonstrated, showing me the third oven.

'Leave an ox-tongue in it overnight,' she told me, 'and it'll be as tender as anything. It'll take you a week though to clean up the dust of the anthracite after they empty the sacks into the cellar. It gets into everything, as far as the hall, even.'

Did this woman want to sell her house or not? we wondered while we admired it and she pointed out the snags.

We had to go. It was time for Harry to be back in hospital.

'Call in the next time you're out. Have a cup of tea and I'll show you the garden. I'm a nut about plants and I have some rare ones.'

As it turned out Mrs Bell was a horticulturist who had won many awards. We did call again but it rained. Instead of the garden she showed us the drawing- and dining-rooms connected or not, as desired, by sliding doors and remarked that the maple floors were easy to keep.

Off the hall were a large study and a spacious cloakroom with

In the kitchen at Orwell Park

yet more cupboard space. If she wasn't selling she would put in a plug for an electric kettle to make the odd cup of tea and to save the trouble of carrying trays up the stairs. We wouldn't mind having tea in the kitchen? At the bottom of the stairs, only about six steps, at right angles to the kitchen she stopped and opened a low door, hardly noticeable in the wall. It revealed a space of about four feet in depth extending as far as we could see.

'It's great for ventilation. I call it the wine-cellar,' she said, smiling. 'Do you go in for wine at all?' she asked.

'We buy the odd bottle when we've friends in,' Harry informed her.

'I do exactly the same myself.' By the satisfaction in her tone, I realised that we had passed a subtle test.

We got talking and we learned that her grandmother had been born in Coalisland, of all places, and that her late husband, although at Trinity and a Protestant, had served in an Irish-speaking battalion during the Emergency. We wondered if her husband and my brother had served together. Still, it was a link. She wanted to know how many children we had. We showed her photographs of them and before we knew where we were it was taken for granted that we were prospective buyers. We learned later that she turned down a more advantageous offer than she quoted to us.

'It's meant for you. It's obvious. That's if you want it.'

The brown paint, the heavy dark curtains and deep pelmets contracting the high, wide bay windows, dissolved before our eyes and left Mrs Bell's personality to pervade the house with generosity and warmth. We moved in the summer of 1956. Mrs Bell left us a hand-tufted Turkish carpet, richly blue and red, on one of the bedroom floors, the carpet on the stairs, the wonderful kitchen table and an assortment of high-quality kitchen and garden tools. Dear Mrs Bell. I think she knew she was selling her house to people who would love it. And we were happy there for nearly twenty-five years.

It was located in the Dartry area convenient to Rathgar village round the corner, Rathmines down the road, to church and schools. Hugo went by bus to CUS (Catholic University School) in Leeson Street, Anna and Kato to Notre Dame des Missions in Churchtown, a short distance away, and, in due course, Peter attended St Mary's in Rathmines.

Keep the mothers occupied

I'm not sure how or why I came to be elected president of the convent school's Parent's Association. I think that at that time I was too busy, and perhaps too tired, to refuse invitations to commitments that I knew in my heart were distractions from more serious personal business.

But the experience revealed the tenor of the times. An enormous amount of effort went into fund-raising to pay for the new school building. An annual garden fête, for example, required prizes for winners of competitions. Had anyone a contact in Clery's or Hector Grey's? Which party-hire firm would lend tables and chairs without charge? Would Premier Dairies give free ice-cream and milk? Who would write to Jacobs for biscuits? And so on.

I suggested to Reverend Mother that a few, say five, professional and business fathers could raise as much money between them as the garden-party, only about £300, without all those time-wasting meetings, arguments, writing of demeaning begging letters, and telephoning. She considered me for a moment.

'I'm afraid you don't understand. You see, Mrs Boylan, the idea is to keep the mothers occupied and to keep them in touch with the school.' I think she suggested that it was the archbishop's idea but, as I am not absolutely sure, I forbear to name him. Intimations of male control were never far away. A Lady Mayer was coming to the school to attend a pupils' concert. She was rich and devoted part of her wealth to the encouragement of music in schools by providing needed instruments. It was a big occasion and, as president of the Parents' Association, I was in the front

Notre Dame des Missions school in Churchtown

line to welcome and present her. I can only suppose that my position gave rise to a tinge of jealousy in the male members of the association because, only two or three days before the concert, I had a phone call.

It was from a pupil's father, a banker.

'I've seen the programme. It can't go out as it is. It's unsuitable for young girls to read. It'll have to be changed.' His tone was peremptory.

Warily, I asked him what he found wrong with it. The nuns had raised no objection. It would be terribly expensive to change it now even if the printers could do it in time.

'There's a word in it that we can't let into the girls' hands.'

I had a vision of a word jumping out of the programmes and dancing from hand to grasping hand.

'A word? What's the word, Mr B.?' I asked, trying to sound placatory.

'Oh, I couldn't possibly say it to a lady, Mrs Boylan. It'll have to go.'

'But I won't be able to do anything about it if I don't know what it is. Don't worry. I'm a married woman with four children. I won't take offence.'

'Illegitimate,' he whispered over the wire.

Apparently, Vivaldi, in the 16th century, opened a refuge for homeless and illegitimate children. No point in telling this anxious father that the good priest-composer had taken a huge risk in setting up the refuge for abandoned children in a society weirdly reminiscent of Ireland in the 1950s.

'I don't think many of the girls will bother to read the notes, Mr B.' I told him. 'If a few bright girls do I'm sure the word will pass them by and if a really clever one wants to know the meaning she just has to be told that it means outside the law.'

I made play with the notion that, as a banker, he wouldn't want to incur the expense of eliminating the word from the programme or of printing new ones especially as the idea was to make money, not to waste it, and I insinuated that his daughter would be the clever one to ask questions. He gave in but not before laying down a law that in future all programmes would have to be vetted by the Parents' Association committee before finalisation.

I rang Reverend Mother to put her in the picture. She was a widely experienced woman, tolerant of human vagaries from having observed them at close quarters. A tiny person, she was one of the mighty army of talented women who joined forces in religious orders and, given the backing of the Church, had set forth to combat disease, ignorance and poverty wherever they found them. She had seen life at its rawest as a prisoner of the Japanese during the war and was now retired from foreign missionary work.

Her reaction to Mr B's complaint was predictable: Do nothing. Human nature hasn't changed since the beginning of time and it'll be the same till the end. She laughed.

'The poor man! But don't cross him. We need him to mind the door at the concert and once he's introduced to Lady Mayer he'll forget his grievance.'

She was a heroic woman and a wise one.

The concert succeeded in earning the school the instruments it needed. The programmes passed scrutiny, if indeed there was any, and the only hitch was Reverend Mother's direction to Mr B. to forbid entry to anyone wearing stiletto heels.

'They can come in barefooted for all I care,' she declared, 'but no stilettos. No use in laying a good floor and having it ploughed up by silly fashion.'

'Ploughed up' was a slight exaggeration but as I had had to cope with numerous stiletto depressions on Mrs Bell's beautiful floors I gave her and Mr B. my enthusiastic support, hoping that a lesson would be learnt before the girls' next party. Stiletto heels were certainly one of the silliest fashions of the century.

Fashion shows were good fund-raisers, however, and one was organised to take place in the Aberdeen Hall in the Gresham Hotel. We needed a prominent person to open it and to attract a crowd. Jack Lynch was Minister for Education and his wife Máirín was admired for her excellent dress sense expressed in Irish fabrics by Irish designers. She was an obvious choice. I was asked to write to her. Would she do us the honour? Goodness me, no! She never spoke in public. Not her place. She wouldn't know what to say. There were dozens of people more qualified than she. She was charmingly modest but we had chosen her for the role and Clare FitzGerald, a fellow member of the committee whose daughter Joan had been one of the first pupils to be enrolled in the school, decided that Mrs Lynch must be persuaded.

Luckily, the FitzGeralds were friends of the Lynches—William O'Brien Fitzgerald SC, was from Cork, like Jack—so Clare invited them to dinner. We could explain to Máirín, she said, that there was nothing to it, a matter of a few sentences. We'd write them for her. All she had to do was to speak them out, loud and clear. Her presence would make all the difference to the show. Give it a bit of style.

We enjoyed an excellent dinner—I remember admiring the salt cellars in the shape of silver swans—and returned to the drawing room for coffee. The men drank their whiskies and, after some general chat, Clare asked Jack to sing. He agreed provided she sang first. Without demur she belted out an old music-hall song,

With Captain Coghlan and Máirín Lynch at the fashion show

'Three Meat Balls', with great good humour. During her performance, Billy, as she called him, smiled benignly at her and beat time with his hand. Good as his word, Jack followed with the Cork anthem, 'The Banks of My Own Lovely Lee'. We all joined in the chorus. Then Jack looked at Máirín. They stood and, very feelingly, sang the duet, 'Home to our Mountain' from the opera, *The Lily of Killarney*.

It was not quite the end of a memorable evening for before we left Máirín agreed that Clare and I should meet her at the school, introduce her to Reverend Mother and the nuns and show her the buildings, the reason for the fund-raising fashion show. In the event she did open the show, most gracefully, made a very good job of her short speech and got due applause.

Grannie's chair

Down through the years, as the children grew, rituals were established. One was the drowning of the shamrock on the 17th of
March, St Patrick's Day. Other people went to the races or to the
dog-show in Ballsbridge or to the country. We went to Clonliffe
Road to drown the shamrock. Woe betide us if we didn't wear a
touch of green; a ribbon, a green tie, sprigs of shamrock, a glittering green and gold harp bought at school—whatever we liked so
long as we honoured the day. As 'Grannie' Mother seemed to
have taken root in the mahogany-framed armchair in the corner
by the fire in the breakfast room. Round her, on the floor and
slung from the arms of the chair, were boxes of various sizes and
wicker baskets and cloth bags. They held every useful thing im-
aginable and some surprises, a packet of flower seeds, maybe, or
new-minted pennies among the buttons, or a cutting from a news-

Peter and Kato watching television in
Orwell Park

paper about someone she'd heard you talk about.

You couldn't imagine a time when Grannie wasn't sitting in that chair or a time when she wouldn't be. The children were so sure of her that the minute the gate was opened, they'd make a wild dash round the side of the house, down the steps through the door, along the flagged passage, through another door and into the room to fling themselves towards the corner. They always stopped in time, though, for they were well warned never, *ever* to touch Grannie's poor legs. She lived with pain. You'd know if you caught her unawares: but she never mentioned it.

'Tch, tch,' she'd say. 'That coat has lost a button.' The offending garment would be handed over. She'd feel for a round yellow Turkish Delight tin and from hundreds in it she'd pick out a button that matched as near as made no difference.

'There might be a thread in that basket,' she'd direct and a few strands of just the right colour would be found wound round a screw of paper. She made us watch to see how she inserted a match between the button and the fabric as she sewed so that the stitches made leeway for the coat to be fastened without dragging. And then she'd stretch the front of the coat and hold it away from her for a good look to make sure it was right . . .

'Keep a thing for seven years and you'll find a use for it,' she'd say, smiling, for hadn't she just shown you?

Mena, Mollie, Nina and I would talk to each other and she talked to the children, bobbing and scuffling around her. Later, in private, one or other of us would catch it.

'A wonder you'd bring the child out in that east wind without his ears covered,' and she'd scrabble in a bag for a woollen cap, intricately knitted. 'Those pants of Hugo's could do with a rest,' was a sharp hint that it was unseemly not to leave a turn in the children's clothes for the needy. But, for now, the drowning of the shamrock was the order of the day. Even now, I feel the fizz in my nose.

I loved the lemonade on St Patrick's Day as I never loved enough 'the dear fingers, so toil-worn for me,' as the song has it. Not that

Mother ever wanted for love. Her sons adored her and never came home without a present for her. She had an admirer, too. Maurice Paul Cullen was an elderly well-to-do cattle trader whose regular visits were, I feel sure, both an annoyance and a secret pleasure to mother. He had left Dungannon when his wife died and had come to Dublin to be near members of his family. He loved to sit by the fire and describe to his old neighbour the places he had visited and the weird and wonderful things he had seen and heard in pursuit of his trade. He was deadly in earnest in his attempts to impress. He demonstrated his experiences by assuming, as he thought, the accents and gestures of the French, Italians, Russians. Once he picked up a tray-cloth and wrapped it round his head in imitation of a Russian orthodox priest, intoning a hymn in a low growl and bowing repeatedly before mother. We slipped from the room and succumbed to hysterical laughter in the kitchen next door.

A visit to Lourdes had, presumably, nothing to do with cattle-trading. He reverently presented mother with a bottle of Lourdes water. He sat with a rosary twined in his fingers and talked about Bernadette and Our Lady as if he had known them all his life. Mother declined his invitation to join his wavering voice in singing the Lourdes hymn, *Ave Maria*. There was no question of her marching with him round the table carrying an imaginary candle and shielding it with a cupped hand from an imaginary wind.

'Any miracles?' Mollie asked him.

'Miracles, miracles,' he said crossly. 'If miracles were two-a-penny there'd be plenty but miracles are hard to come by. There's many a miracle nobody's heard about and there's many a one claimed that never happened.'

Mena and I looked after Mother in her last illness, so gallantly borne. Two more of her sons had died: Kevin, the youngest in the family, had a heart condition undiagnosed when he joined the army during 'the Emergency'. He was invalided out after a collapse during a route march. He apparently recovered, joined the

Rank film organisation in London and was happily married when he died suddenly of a heart attack in 1953. He was only thirty-three years old. Phauds died in his sleep, at home in Clonliffe Road in 1954; he, too, had suffered from a heart condition.

It was 1960. Other members of the family had been summoned and were about the house but only I was with her when she died. She was eighty-five. Her eyes, which had been fogged by exhaustion, became crystal clear. She asked me to open the window and I understood that this was the old Irish way, to let her spirit fly free. I held her hands and she gave me a message.

'Tell them all I loved each one of you equally.' And then, with great emphasis, '*and your darling father.*'